HOW TO GO FROM RAGS TO RICHES IN REAL ESTATE

D1528435

HOW TO GO
TO
IN REAL

William Dooner with William Proctor

FROM RAGS RICHES ESTATE

A Guide to Turning Depressed,

Neglected, or Little-Known

Property Investments into

Millions in the 1980's

WILLIAM MORROW AND COMPANY, INC.
New York   1982

Library of Congress Cataloging in Publication Data

Dooner, William.
  How to go from rags to riches in real estate.

  1. Real estate investment. I. Proctor, William,
1941–   . II. Title.
HD1382.5.D66   332.63'24   82–2201
ISBN 0–688–00998–0   AACR2

Printed in the United States of America

First Edition

1 2 3 4 5 6 7 8 9 10

BOOK DESIGN BY BERNARD SCHLEIFER

To my wife, Ellie, and to the wonderful fellowship of recovered alcoholics who continue to share their experiences, strength and hope with me.

CONTENTS

HOW TO GO FROM RAGS TO RICHES IN REAL ESTATE

1

From Rags...

I STARTED OUT at the absolute bottom of the barrel.

My early life, as the second son of poor Irish immigrants in the East Harlem district of Manhattan, was filled with violence and crime. As a teenager, I had become a confirmed alcoholic. Because I couldn't hold down a job more than a couple of months, I often had to supplement my income by selling my blood to New York City hospitals.

Yet today, everything is different. I'm a family man with a great wife and five wonderful kids. I no longer drink anything stronger than a soda. And I've long since made my first million.

How did such a dramatic change take place in my life?

That's a long story—a story that will unfold in more detail as we move through the various topics in this book. But for now, let me just say that in my case the secret of moving from rags to riches was unlocked by two "master keys" of real estate investment:

• First of all, I learned some practical principles about how to transform poor properties into big profit-making investments, which catapulted me from a *minus* net worth to *millions* in real estate holdings in just a few years.

● Secondly, I discovered some psychological and spiritual principles that enabled me to get my personal life in order and, consequently, to release some important natural business abilities that had long been suppressed.

These two keys to success—the practical and the personal—are intimately interconnected, and I'll be referring to both regularly as we get further into our discussion. Taken together, they comprise the foundation for what I call the "property personality," or a body of personal traits and talents that can enable you to turn a poor piece of real estate into an unbelievably profitable investment.

But I want to make it clear, right here at the beginning, that I recognize that you and I are different people. I started out with a special set of personal problems, which I wouldn't wish on anyone else, and so what worked for me may not be quite right in many ways for you.

At the same time, I firmly believe there are certain broad principles that apply to effective living in general and to effective real estate investment in particular. It's those fundamentals that will emerge in the form of clearcut guidelines for action as we discuss actual situations involving both successful and unsuccessful property deals.

Finally, perhaps the most practical set of things I'll have to say, from the viewpoint of the average reader, centers on the answer to this question: "What's the best kind of real estate investment in an uncertain or bad economy?"

As I write these words, we're in the midst of what almost any sane economist or business expert would call a "bad" economy. And for the last few years, as well as for the foreseeable future, we have faced and will continue to face what must, at best, be called an "uncertain" economic outlook. The rules of the real estate game are changing quickly to meet the new challenges. So if you hope to preserve your property assets *and* have a chance to build them into millions, it's absolutely necessary that you understand the new approaches to investment and know the best ways you can use them to go from "rags to riches" in record time.

Now, let's focus for a moment on the word *rags*. I like that word because it's symbolic of my own early life. That's how I started out, in a worthless, tattered condition. And it's also the way a lot of real estate—potentially the *best* real estate—starts out. For if you look closely at the rags of property around you, you may well find in them the seeds for a real estate fortune. So in this book, we're going to concentrate on depressed, neglected and overlooked property investments—real "down and out" cases. We'll discuss how to find this property, how to build it up and then how to sell it for incredible multiples of its original value.

This approach to property investment is the specialty I've been developing during more than two decades in business, and it's a specialty that has made me and a few others fortunes, which continue to grow in good times as well as in bad. But to understand how the rags-to-riches approach can work for you, it's necessary for you to know a little more about the kind of personal traits that can pave the way to success in this type of real estate investment in today's uncertain market.

To introduce some of these special traits, I have to fall back on the experiences I know best—my own ventures in real estate and life. So, even at the risk of seeming immodest, I want to spend a few pages offering my own development into an entrepreneur as a case study for your consideration.

* * *

This is a very personal and sometimes painful story: an account of where I came from; what I've learned about real estate investment, including techniques for strengthening my own innate weaknesses and building on my entrepreneurial strengths; and where I think the biggest profit centers of property will be in the future. My own personal rags-to-riches narrative begins in an unlikely place—in a rough tenement in East Harlem.

I was born around 104th Street and Madison Avenue in East Harlem in 1931. Both my parents were from Ireland, and Manhattan's upper East Side in those days was the home for a lot of Irish immigrants. Our neighborhood was also heavily Jewish and Italian; the Puerto Ricans who live there now didn't start arriving in heavy numbers until a decade or so later.

By any standard, we were poor. Before I was eleven years old, we had lived in at least eight run-down tenements, including some cold-water flats, and there never seemed to be enough money for me to have the basic necessities that go with a normal kid's life. We were dispossessed several times by our landlords because we couldn't pay the rent. I remember coming home from school one day and finding all our furniture on the sidewalk. My father, like many other men in those Depression years, often couldn't find work. When jobs were available, he worked as a laborer, longshoreman, bartender or poolroom helper.

So I began to develop my innate entrepreneurial instincts at a young age. Some of them were just on this side of the law, some of them on the other. But they all helped keep my pockets full of enough change to allow me to buy the drinks, hot dogs, movies and other things that kept me reasonably satisfied as a kid.

For example, one of the ways I made money was to sell

flowers on the street. Another way was to shine shoes in
Third Avenue taverns. But there were also "business ventures" that were on the shadier side: For two years, I ran
numbers for a bookie who also operated an ice and coal
business. I learned to keep from getting "busted" by the
cops through a technique of memorizing the multidigit
numbers rather than writing them down on my arm or on
a piece of paper. If the police stopped me, they could
search all they liked, but they wouldn't find any evidence
or "policy" slips. Some people have speculated that my
ability to carry a lot of figures around in my head as an
adult can be traced back to that early street training in the
East Harlem underworld.

At age nine I also had a job siphoning off fermented
cider from barrels in a tavern which was owned by two
women who sold more than drink in their place. My
heavy drinking started at about this time. I would take a
few swigs myself before I handed the cider over to the
women, and many times I'd go to school a little high—
even though I was only in the third grade.

My business interests in those days were definitely
"diversified" in the sense that I got into anything, legal or
illegal, so long as it would turn a profit. And I soon found
that those things that had the highest profit potential
were often related in some way to real estate.

I don't know exactly what it is about land that makes
it such a lucrative base for building a fortune. Perhaps it's
the fact that there is relatively little of it in prime locations. So if you own or have an interest in some property
in a reasonably good place, the chances are the demand
for it will grow in the near future—perhaps in ways you
could never foresee when you made your original purchase.

Or it may be that there is something about having a
piece of property as a base of operations, a stable center

for personal investments and broader business dealings, that enhances a person's chances of turning a modest investment stake into millions.

Whatever the reason, some of the most lucrative business and investment ventures seem to revolve around real estate. Long before I became a teenager, I learned this important principle in my wheeling and dealing on the tough streets of New York City around Second and Third Avenues.

Many of the buildings in our part of Harlem were being condemned at about this time. They had been earmarked to be torn down, and all the legitimate tenants had moved out. When I was barely in grammar school, I spent hours looking at those vacant structures and poking around in them, and, gradually, rags-to-riches ideas began to form in my brain.

For example, by watching the older kids and adults in the neighborhood, I learned a number of ways to turn what remained of the wood and metal in those buildings into big bucks—at least big for a seven-year-old. On many a cold winter day, with a single-headed hand ax tucked under my coat, I would find an out-of-the-way room and start chopping up the pine floorboards. Then I'd put the planks and kindling into large potato sacks and go out to canvass the neighborhood for tenants who might want to buy some firewood. As it turned out, there were many people who were eager to purchase my wares at the low prices I was offering—about twenty-five cents for a half bag of pine floor wood. They used the wood for coal-burning stoves right in their apartments.

On many of these trips, my brother would be with me, and we would climb the inside walls of a tenement that was just a "shell" in the sense that the steel superstructure had been removed. Often, these walls were known to fall and kill others who were browsing around the property.

But wood wasn't the only commodity I learned to capitalize on in those old, abandoned buildings. Every piece of land you encounter has a variety of uses that can make you a pile of money. It's just a matter of looking hard enough at the property, studying it thoroughly and then relating what it has to offer to what public demand is on the outside.

So I began to focus in on "BX" cable in those buildings. This was copper wire which was wrapped up in some sort of black tape that was used for insulation. The manufacturer then inserted the entire bundle into a zinc casing called "BX" cable.

I knew that plenty of copper wiring was buried in the buildings because I had come across it while chopping up walls and floorboards to get my firewood. And I was also aware that some Second Avenue junk shops and other metal dealers were quite interested in buying the copper. So I put two and two together and decided to expand my business interests into metal salvage.

Of course, knocking down the walls to get to the cables was dangerous. In some cases, Con Edison, the electric power company, had left the electricity on, and the wires were alive. Sometimes, I'd chop into the cable and blow the fuses for the remaining tenants. But I learned how to make jumpers to put into the electric boxes to by-pass the electricity. This could be done with a four-inch piece of insulated copper which I would install in the fuse box to by-pass the electric meter.

On many days I was able to extract twenty feet or more of the BX cable out of the building. Then, I took it outside, built a little fire against the street curb next to the building and threw the wire into the flames to burn off the insulation. After this procedure, the copper was exposed and ready to sell, and I was able to get so much per pound for it from the junk shops in the neighborhood.

Now, I realize that this kind of low-level salvage operation that I was involved in as a kid isn't what you'd normally consider when you think about how to make money in real estate. But the point is that there are many ways to skin a cat in making money out of a piece of property.

The important thing for anyone who wants to make a fortune in real estate these days is to learn to escape the old, traditional ways of looking at land and buildings and enter a new dimension of entrepreneurial thinking. A piece of property often isn't what it seems to be at first glance. Always look again, and try to imagine as many ways as possible of getting every possible dollar and cent out of that land and those buildings on it.

You'll have to discard most of the money-making ideas that pop into your head—there's no doubt about that. But if you give your fantasies free rein for a while, you'll find that several concepts will probably stand up to close scrutiny. Those are the ones that you should act upon.

One of the most important principles of property investment that I learned in those days as a youngster on the streets of New York was that you have to "sell your head" —or learn to turn your ideas and abilities into money— before you start investing in big capital assets. In other words, many people think that the only way you can establish a big capital base or a personal fortune is to go out and purchase an expensive piece of property first and then figure out how to make a profit out of it. But that's doing things backwards.

So instead of trying to acquire the physical things first, it's important at the outset to find out how to generate the income and seed money. For example, if you want to build a restaurant, I think it's important to learn first how to be a dishwasher, or at least establish a partnership with someone who knows, before you buy a tract of land and erect a building. This is just another way of saying that you should learn the business from the ground up before you invest your savings in real estate that you may not be able to convert into cash because you lack basic business skills.

Another business principle I learned even before I was a teenager—a principle that also helped me later on in my real estate investments—was how to deal with competition.

One of the ways I learned this lesson was by selling newspapers in Manhattan. I'd buy forty or fifty copies of the New York *Daily News* and then hustle up Third Avenue with the papers under one arm and my shoeshine box over one shoulder. I always made sure I was the first kid on the route—that was the first thing I learned. Then, I'd go in and out of the bars, shining shoes and selling newspapers.

When I'd walked about a mile up one side of the avenue—that's about twenty blocks in New York—I'd cross over and head back down the other side. Sometimes, though, I'd run into bars that already had newspapers, and then I knew I had a problem: I had a competitor.

Sometimes, of course, it just wasn't possible to avoid competition, and so it had to be confronted. For me as a kid in those days, that usually meant a threat or a fight. If you didn't fight, then you had to forget that territory the next day. If you just ran away or avoided a confrontation, the other guy assumed you weren't around any more and he took over your territory permanently. You can only do that so often before you run out of turf, and so it's necessary to take a stand sooner than later if the competition seems to be building up against you.

This simple little principle I learned as a kid has been extremely important as I've become involved in real estate deals. Many times, the person who invests in property on the side, in addition to his regular business interests, completely ignores how important it is to be a tough competitor in his real estate ventures. It's almost as though he regards his attempts to make money in land as something completely separate from making money in other fields.

It's important to avoid such counterproductive thinking, especially if you hope to take a neglected or depressed piece of property and make a profit out of it. Turning a "sow's ear" of real estate into a "silk purse" takes some creativity and perseverance, which may well involve coming up with new ways to compete effectively for the real estate dollars that are floating around in our economy. It's always important to think in terms of buying property with the intention of becoming an effective competitor so that you can eventually sell or lease it for a profit.

So as a general rule, you can't buy land and then just sit on it and expect to make a profit. You have to think of techniques to exploit your property investment aggressively, in a way that creates more demand for your real estate than for that owned by the guy next door.

There's nothing basically immoral about this competitive approach, of course. At its essence, it's just a matter of using your native skills and marketing creativity to the utmost. As a matter of fact, to demonstrate just how moral and desirable hard work and healthy competition in the marketplace are, I like to refer to the approach Jesus often took in his teachings. In Matthew 25:14–30, for example, he told an especially instructive parable about business.

In that story, a landowner entrusted his property, or "talents," to three servants just before he went on a long journey. Two of them got out into the marketplace and traded effectively with their capital, so that they ended up with ten and four talents respectively. And they were praised highly and given greater responsibilities when their boss returned.

But the third sat on his holdings. When the master

returned, he reported, "Master, I knew you to be a hard man, reaping where you did not sow, and gathering where you did not winnow; so I was afraid, and I went and hid your talent in the ground. Here you have what is yours."

But the master rejected this servant, saying, "You wicked and slothful servant! . . . you ought to have invested my money with the bankers, and at my coming I should have received what was my own with interest. So take the talent from him and give it to the one who has the ten talents. For to every one who has will more be given, and he will have abundance; but from him who has not, even what he has will be taken away."

The point for us here is that it's essential to take the abilities and capital assets you have and multiply them as much as you honestly can in the marketplace. If you don't use what you have, you'll lose it, whether in the spiritual or temporal realm. And I've found that this principle applies to real estate holdings and ventures as much as to any other investment.

Another important business principle, which I learned as a kid and which was to have a decisive impact on my approach to real estate later in life, was to accumulate capital systematically through seemingly worthless investments.

For example, I noticed at a Greek floral market on the West Side that by late Saturday afternoon some of the flowers, like the gardenias and roses, were right on the verge of wilting or falling apart. The owners of the market were in the habit of throwing these flowers away instead of putting them in ice-box refrigeration. So I immediately asked myself, "Is there any way I can make a profit off those flowers?"

Finally, an idea came to mind, and it kept me in pocket change for several years: I bought those flowers for a penny or two apiece, and then I made corsages out of them. I got into the habit of carrying in my shoeshine box a little pair of scissors, some soft wire and other materials that I could use to fix the flowers up. Then, I arranged and displayed them on a big piece of cardboard that had holes punched in it for the stems. Finally, I'd walk up and down Broadway every Saturday night selling those flowers for a quarter or fifty cents apiece.

But there was one other step in this entrepreneurial process that was just as important as earning the money: At the end of the day, even though I had a pocketful of dough, I'd hitch all the way home on the back fender of a bus instead of paying the seven-cent fare. Why? Because I wanted to conserve my hard-earned capital for another venture, not blow it impulsively on expenses I didn't consider essential.

And you know what? Even if you deal in millions of dollars in real estate transactions, the principles are no different. I've heard highly successful investors say, "Well, the only difference between the money earned by a kid selling papers on the street and the multimillionaire selling a shopping center is the size of the numbers." And I'm convinced that statement is absolutely true.

So these were some of the fundamental business traits that were ingrained in me at an early age and that became the foundation for my later career in real estate. I think it's important to emphasize again at this point that it's a serious mistake to separate basic business expertise from the kind of expertise it takes to turn a poor piece of land into a big money-maker.

In fact, the skills required to make it big in real estate are often *exactly* what it takes to make it in any kind of business—especially entrepreneurial kinds of ventures. The top-flight real estate investor has learned to look into the *hidden heart* of a piece of property and see its potential and essential worth in a way that the uninformed and inexperienced person can't do.

If you had seen me wandering around the streets of New York City, wearing my old clothes and maybe sporting a black eye from my latest fight, you'd probably have been tempted to discount my potential in the business world almost without a second thought. But if you could have probed my mind and heart in a little more depth, you might well have come to a different, more favorable conclusion about my future prospects.

But I don't want to give the impression that the seeds of *all* my real-estate abilities and skills were sown while I was still a youngster in East Harlem. On the contrary, I was lacking something absolutely essential to success, something that I can only express through a word like *character.*

When I talk about character, I'm not referring only to personal morality and uprightness, though I could have used a good dose of those virtues when I was a kid. No, what I'm describing is something that includes those things but goes much deeper—perhaps a trait that one of my early mentors called grim determination, or a powerful drive toward some vision or goal, or maybe what others have called an ultimate purpose in life.

I had certain qualities that on the surface may have passed for character; but in actuality they were something else. I was highly competitive and ready to fight to hold my "business territory" as a hustling street kid. But that was mainly because I was pugnacious and cocky by nature, not because I had such deep convictions about the value of what I was doing. I was always ready for a fight if I felt threatened or challenged.

Also, I seemed to have a lot of perseverance and ingenuity when I came up with all those business schemes and implemented them. But as Plato and others have said, "Necessity is the mother of invention," and necessity is exactly what was motivating me. My family was short on money, and if I wanted to cover my expenses and buy enough extra food to reach my "minimum daily requirements," I had to go out and earn a few extra bucks. Nothing particularly high-flown or noble about that!

So I'll admit it: Even though I was developing some solid skills on one level, I lacked the character development at that early age to have the staying power that is required to succeed in life, much less in real estate investment. The major result of this deficiency—a result that almost brought me to an early death—was alcoholism.

Although I'd sometimes take a few drinks while I was still in grammar school stealing cider from those female tavern owners and grabbing a stray drink when I could in Third Avenue bars, I really started to drink heavily when I was about fourteen years old. In my Irish neighborhood, drinking was a way of life. When a kid graduated from grammar school and he was barely in his teens, his family held a "beer racket," or party. All his uncles and other relatives came in from Friday through Sunday, and usually there were many bottles of rye whiskey available on the kitchen table. In the back of the old railroad-flat tenement, there was also a barrel of beer.

The kids were allowed to drink freely at those parties. If a boy indicated he wanted a swig, the adults would just say, "Go ahead!" With violins and Irish songs going steadily in the background, the event usually turned into a real bash with plenty of fistfights.

So we got smashed. Booze was an accepted drink for all, adults and kids alike. You got into the habit of heavy drinking, not only at those parties but anytime during the day or evening, whether on weekends or in the middle of the week.

My first job after high school was with the Borden Company in New York City, where I worked as a law clerk. I got paid the minimum wage, about $80 every two weeks, or maybe $65 in take-home pay. Although I was drinking pretty heavily at the time, it was impossible to maintain a respectable booze habit on that kind of money. Beer was ten cents a glass in those days, and a hard shot of whiskey in a neighborhood bar was about forty cents an ounce. Also there was a pretty girl I was going with at the time.

So I began to hock everything I could lay my hands on—my watch, family toasters, my brother's suits, everything—at the local pawnshop on Third Avenue. I also took to stealing things, such as clocks and furniture from apartment lobbies, and sold them to get extra money.

I can still remember a loveseat I took from one building. It was about five o'clock in the morning, and I managed to get it out onto the corner of Madison Avenue and Ninety-fifth Street. Then, I rolled it on the sidewalk down to Third Avenue, to Hungarian Steve's used-furniture shop.

Of course, I got there well before he opened, and by the time he arrived at nine o'clock, he found me sleeping outside his door in this loveseat. I was sure I was going to get a good price for it, but all he did was take one look at it and say, "Get that piece of junk out of here!"

That was one of the biggest disappointments of my life. All I had wanted was five or ten bucks to keep my current drunk going, but I ended up with nothing but a worthless piece of furniture.

As you can imagine, this kind of extracurricular activity didn't enhance my productivity at work very much. I had been attending St. John's University on a program that was supported by the Borden Company, but I just used my connection with the school as an excuse to take time off to do more drinking. In fact, I used almost any excuse I could dream up to get more time to spend in local bars.

One day, I walked into the office, and Hilda, a woman I worked with, walked over with this concerned look on her face. "How was your EKG?" she asked.

"What are you talking about?" I asked.

"Your heart attack. You called in yesterday and said you'd had a heart attack."

Here I was, a nineteen-year-old kid, and I had actually phoned in with the excuse that I had a coronary. Of course, I didn't remember anything about the call.

I soon got fired by the Borden Company because of chronic absenteeism, which was the result of chronic alcoholism. Then a string of other jobs ensued, and I lost them all because I cared for the bottle more than I cared for anything or anyone else.

But a spotty, ineffectual employment record wasn't my only problem. I also started getting into trouble with the law. I was arrested at least eight times during my late teens and early twenties, mostly on charges relating to my drinking. One time I tore up a Madison Avenue bar and in the process put my hand through a jukebox.

I also fought with cops whenever they got in my way, and on one occasion a couple of policemen started shooting at me when I was trying to escape from them after I had attacked a cabdriver. That time, I talked the prosecutor out of recommending my case for an indictment by swearing on a Bible that I'd never take another drink in New York City. Needless to say, I broke this pledge but I still succeeded in avoiding an indictment on the charge.

By the time I reached my early twenties, my health had started to fall apart. I had been selling my blood to

New York hospitals to get drinking money. I can even remember one time that I sold blood out of my left arm at the Bellevue Blood Bank for five dollars and then went right out to a local bar and drank it up. Within an hour, I had hitched a ride on the back bumper of a bus, just like I used to do as a kid, and rode uptown to another hospital to sell some more blood out of the other arm and buy some more drinks.

Finally, I was admitted to the Rockefeller Institute for Medical Research as a research subject. The only way you could get in there was to be a "specimen." You had to have an unusually advanced case of alcoholism, and by any test, I was quite advanced.

By this time I knew I needed serious help. My health was so bad that sometimes I sensed I was close to death. My personal finances were so messed up that half the time I didn't know where my next drink was coming from, and I rarely got around to paying any of the bills that kept accumulating.

At one point—and in many ways, for me, this was the nadir of my life—I actually stole some money from my mother. She had given me a few dollars to pay our gas and electric bill, but I used it to buy myself drinks. As I downed one glass of liquor after another that day, it dawned on me what I had done. The impact of my act was so great, I felt so rotten, that I didn't get drunk, even though I had been drinking for about ten or twelve hours. I knew I had reached the end of the line then. I had really hit bottom. It was a matter of doing something to save myself now or never having a chance to become a decent person.

So I joined a fellowship of recovered alcoholics who helped me turn myself around. It was at this point that I really began to develop *character*—the kind I needed to release the talents for business, and especially for real estate investment, that I had begun to develop as a young-ster but that had been buried deep inside as a result of my addiction to booze.

Except for one slipup with the bottle, which landed me on Chicago's skid row in 1955, I haven't touched a drop of alcohol in more than twenty-five years. I can only attribute the transformation inside myself to the work of God, and I believe that over the years an acknowledg-ment of the priority of God in my life, and more recently of a specific commitment to Jesus Christ, has been the key to the grim determination—the sense of purpose and the strength to persevere in tough times—that has resulted in my financial success.

Now, as I said at the outset of this personal history, I don't think it's necessary for everyone to take the same route I've taken to become a success in business. And I certainly don't believe that the personal qualities and strengths I may have acquired over the years are charac-teristics you *have* to possess to transform depressed and neglected property opportunities into millions. But I do believe that it's essential to develop some sort of stable center to your personality—what I've called character—in order to have the staying power it takes to turn rags into riches in real estate.

In fact a strong character of this sort is the cornerstone of what I called at the beginning of this discussion the property personality, or that body of traits that can en-hance the success of any real estate career—especially one that focuses on building up *poor* properties.

But a solid set of personal strengths is not enough to enable you to transform a poor piece of land or a decrepit building. No, these real estate "rags" must themselves harbor certain key seeds of growth and possibilities for exploitation if you want to make a respectable profit in today's real estate market.

So now let's get down to some of the specifics about where you can find poor property with powerful potential in the current economy—and also what profitable action you can take with that property after you identify it.

2

Where to Find
Poor Property
with Potential

THE FIRST THING to remember when you set out to find depressed or neglected property that you hope to transform into a big profit maker is that *you shouldn't feel limited solely by geographical location.*

In other words, you may hear one self-appointed expert say, "You can't go wrong if you buy property in Dallas." Or, "Long Island real estate is underpriced now. Buy a piece of land anywhere in Suffolk or Nassau counties and you're bound to make a bundle within ten years."

The problem with this sort of advice is that it tackles the issue of real estate investment from a completely wrong-headed perspective. Geography is often a factor in a wise person's decision to purchase property, but it's only *one* factor. As a result, it's almost impossible to make any broad generalizations about one part of the country being preferable to another. A more productive kind of approach is to examine each section of a region, a state and even a city in detail to determine whether there are particular tracts that can fit into a business concept that will allow you to exploit those tracts.

Nonetheless, I believe there are a few reasonably

meaningful general remarks that can be made about the real estate potential of certain sections of the country.

First of all, in my opinion the Deep South and the Sun Belt offer the most promising potential in the foreseeable future for turning neglected or depressed property into a fortune. I'm talking about places like South Carolina, Georgia, the panhandle of Florida (from Panama City west) and large chunks of all the southern states west of Georgia out to Arizona.

In contrast, sections like the Northeast and California are now and will continue to be less attractive for a rags-to-riches approach to real estate investment.

It's important to remember, however, that every generalization like these has its exceptions. Even if you buy some property in Georgia, there's no guarantee, regardless of what you do with it, that it's going to appreciate significantly in value, even in the next fifty years. You have to have a good business idea and then let that idea guide you to the right kind of property.

Similarly, even though the Northeast may offer fewer real estate opportunities as a whole than the Sun Belt, that doesn't mean that you can't make big money investing in some sections of that region—but again, you've got to have the right business approach.

For example, the housing market on Long Island tends to be depressed as this book is going to press. Some sections of the Island, especially some of the poorer, physically unattractive residential areas that are a relatively long distance from the Long Island Rail Road, will probably stay depressed for a while.

But I predict that some of the residential areas near the coasts, and especially those coastal areas with good beaches, will go up significantly in value within the next five years, or at least as soon as mortgage money becomes more available. Also, middle-income housing in stable or upwardly mobile residential districts within walking distance or a short drive of the railroad to New York City will also likely increase in value as more people with families elect to escape the exorbitantly high rents of Manhattan.

I also hear many "experts" telling people to stay away from property investments in big urban areas like New York City because of the relative volatility of housing prices there. There's a lot to be said for this advice. But like everything else in the real estate business, you have to examine such generalizations quite closely just to be sure there is no way you can capitalize on one of the exceptions to the rule.

Take the South Bronx, for example. That's supposed to be one of the worst residential sections in the country and, in the view of many, perhaps one of the worst places in the world as a potential real estate investment. But if you have the right people and the right approach, you may find it's not such a bad place for your money after all.

I was deeply involved in advising new minority business ventures during the "black capitalism" surge in the 1960s, and I also worked with depressed business enterprises in Northern Ireland in the 1970s. So I have some ideas about what will work to turn seemingly hopeless ghetto real estate into a money-making proposition. Here's a possible scenario that could make even the uninviting, neglected turf of the South Bronx a viable real estate investment.

I learned the hard way that the best cure for an alcoholic must come from within. The same thing is true for a depressed ghetto like the South Bronx. You may be able to move from the outside into Oak Ridge, Tennessee, and buy a neglected motel, as I did a few years ago, and then turn it into a multimillion-dollar property—as I also did.

But that approach won't work in an area where you have blocks and blocks of neglected real estate and pover-

ty-level residents. In this kind of "bombed-out" district—
as they call the South Bronx because many of the buildings have been burned and otherwise damaged so that
they actually look as though they've been through a series
of air raids—the residents themselves have to take the
initiative in transforming their property.

Of course, this doesn't mean that much of the money
and expertise can't come from the outside. It's just that
the *leadership* for any real estate project must come from
within the community. The people who live there know
their neighbors and they are intimately familiar with the
local problems. They have not only a vested economic but
also a social and ethnic interest, and that's what it takes
in a ghetto area. As a result, they have an innate understanding of the problems that they are likely to face. And
most important of all, they have more staying power to
see the project through to the end, even when the going
gets especially rough.

Property in these depressed urban areas, even in New
York City, is dirt cheap. With as little as $40,000, you can
get the ball rolling for a good real estate deal. But as I've
already said, you have to have the right business idea
before you buy the real estate.

So suppose you presently work in a company that
manufactures wallpaper, and you determine that many
people would be willing to buy bright, cheery wallpaper
for their apartments if it were cheap enough. You're also
aware that manufacturing wallpaper is a labor-intensive
industry, and you know that unemployment is a big problem in the South Bronx. So you put two and two together
and decide that you would probably have no trouble hiring people to work in a wallpaper factory in that area if
you could just set one up.

The next step—which is both the most important and
may be the most difficult—is to make contact with people

who live in the South Bronx and bring them in as participants in your concept. But actually, if you're involved in
community work or a church that involves a good cross
section of New Yorkers, it may not be so hard after all. For
example, you might make contact with church members
or community leaders whom you know in the South
Bronx, and they in turn would put you in touch with the
people you need to know to get your venture off the
ground.

So before you know it, you could have a nucleus for a
solid little wallpaper factory: the person or people with
the capital outlay of $40,000; the one who has experience
with a wallpaper manufacturer; a bookkeeper; a salesperson who knows the neighborhoods in the market where
you want to concentrate your sales pitch; and a personnel
manager with a few willing workers who are ready to start
manufacturing wallpaper.

But you may be wondering by now, what does all this
have to do with real estate investment? The answer is that
it has *everything* to do with it. You can't start a business
like this in a large metropolitan area unless you have a
solid real estate base from which to operate. Either you
have to lease space at relatively high rents or you have to
buy a building. And in this case, I think a purchase would
be the best way to go—for several reasons.

For one thing, property is so cheap in areas like the
South Bronx that if you can do *anything* to improve its
value, you probably will be able to make a good profit in
just a few years on the real estate alone. And setting up
a viable manufacturing company in a previously "bombed
out" or abandoned building in a low-income neighborhood will go a long way toward enticing other business
enterprises to follow your lead and come into the area as
well. I know this will work because I've seen it happen in
black capitalism enterprises in the Midwest and also in

clothing factories that employ out-of-work Catholic youths in Belfast and Londonderry, Northern Ireland.

Also, when you purchase property in a ghetto area for the purpose of encouraging local business interests, you automatically set yourself up to qualify for all sorts of government breaks and benefits. For example, in New York City, you'd be in a position to negotiate for a suspension of property tax assessments—say for five years, until you got your business on its feet. The local government in many cities wants to clean up the slum areas enough to agree to an arrangement like this. After all, in a place like the South Bronx, they're not getting paid taxes on many of the buildings now anyway. So it would be in the government's interest to give a tax incentive to get a new business started, because eventually taxes *will* be paid if the venture is successful.

It's also possible to go to the federal government for small-business loans and minority aid with a project like this, and many other forms of aid may be available. So with one good idea, it may well be possible to pick what looks like the worst property in town and still turn it into a fortune.

The main point of this particular example is to demonstrate that while geography may be of some importance in determining your chances for successful real estate investment, it's by no means a controlling consideration. In the final analysis, it's not so important where you live in this country, because you probably are already sitting on a real estate gold mine of some sort. Some areas, like the Sun Belt, may have more such opportunities, and that's why it's best to look first in those areas if you live near them. But if you live in New York or New England, there are still plenty of ways you can find poor property with the seeds of a fortune hidden in it. It's just a matter of putting the right idea together with the right piece of real estate.

So far, we've been considering some of the pros and cons of broad geographical regions for successful rags-to-riches real estate investment. But it's also important to narrow your focus to your particular locality so that you learn to distinguish between different tracts and types of property within a single city or even a single neighborhood.

For example, your chances of making a big profit on a land investment may be greater in the Florida panhandle, around Fort Walton Beach, than they are in upstate New York. But you can still be a failure in Florida—or a success in New York—depending on how well you understand the money-making potential for certain types of land in those specific areas.

Now, let's spend a few moments concentrating on the advantages and disadvantages of different kinds of well-known and not so well-known approaches to land use and ownership that are available these days in many localities around the country.

The single-family house In my opinion, the single-family house will soon be a thing of the past. One school of thought these days says, "Go buy a single-family house, no matter what the mortgage rates are. Why? Because it's going to be cheaper now than it will be later."

The problem with this view is that it's based on certain assumptions about inflation that may not be true in the future. Inflation may go up at a double-digit rate, but then again it may not. Or if it does go up, it doesn't necessarily follow that real estate prices will also go up across the board. As a matter of fact, they may go down, as has happened in some sections of the country recently, even though the inflation rate has stayed high.

Finally, the worst scenario of all may occur: You may lock yourself into a higher mortgage rate than you can maintain at your present salary, but then how do you pay it if we face some sort of monetary or economic collapse and you lose your job? Or perhaps you may hold on to your job, but you have to accept a pay rollback or at best no raises for a couple of years while your company tries to survive the bad economic conditions. Then you may become a slave to that house, putting every extra cent you have into your monthly payments to avoid losing the property. And in the end, you may not be able to keep up, and the lender will have to foreclose.

Of course, if you can afford to fit a certain mortgage payment into your budget and you want a home for convenience sake rather than as an investment, a single-family house may be just the thing for you. Also, there is at least one major exception to these problems with single-family homes, which I'll describe in more detail later: That's the run-down house in a good or upwardly mobile neighborhood that you move into and immediately fix up for resale. Although I believe the profit potential is more limited with this approach to real estate investment than with other ways I'll be describing, you can still make some money this way. But in general, it's best to look elsewhere for a good investment in real estate.

Duplexes, triplexes and condominium complexes Multifamily housing strikes me as being the wave of the future. Florida was a major birthplace for this approach to real estate, and the concept has crawled up into other states in the Southeast and the Sun Belt. I'm convinced it's going to become more popular in other parts of the country as well.

Condominium and townhouse complexes are also growing quickly in popularity because people are finding they enjoy having someone else take care of expensive, time-consuming maintenance and also having access to sports facilities, like tennis courts, that they might not be able to buy on their own. I own a single-family home, but I've also purchased a condominium and land for another residence in a cooperative development in upstate Georgia. These dwellings are located in a beautiful wooded area that offers a variety of golf, swimming and tennis facilities. My family uses the condominium for weekend relaxation occasionally, but the main reason I got into it was that I feel it's a good investment for the future. Owning two or three condominium units in a well-run complex will, in my opinion, be a much better investment ten years from now than owning a larger single-family dwelling for the same price.

I wouldn't be surprised if, in about ten years, people are saying, "Condominiums, duplexes and triplexes are here! Forget the single-family house! Are you kidding? Who owns a single-family house anymore?"

Suburban real estate The profit potential of anything you buy in the suburbs, more than almost any other type of real estate investment, is going to depend on geography. And the two keys to suburban ownership are (1) the growth potential of the adjacent urban area, and (2) the tax bite the local government takes out of homeowners.

By these tests, I would say that a city like Tampa, Florida, would be a much better place to invest in suburban real estate than, say, Westchester County, New York. Tampa is a growing city, while New York City has leveled off and in some respects is even declining in business growth. Also, property taxes and other local taxes are much lower in the Tampa area than in the New York City suburbs.

Beachfront property This is an excellent investment, almost anywhere you look. The farther south you go, the better your eventual property potential.

Farmland Developed farmland can be a good investment, but unlike the situation a decade or more ago, you have to shop very carefully to get the most mileage out of your money.

I recall back in the late fifties that farmland in the heart of Illinois was selling at $700 an acre. I was in business in that area then, and I recall advising my father-in-law, who was a farmer, "You know, you really ought to buy more of this property here at seven hundred dollars because I think some day we're going to be feeding the world."

That land is now worth about $4,000 an acre, and that part of Illinois could legitimately be called "the breadbasket of the world."

But it was easier to pinpoint big potential in farmland in those days because the nation was about to go through an economic boom in which the farmers would participate. Now things are different. Personally, even though there is some good farmland still out there, I wouldn't touch a farm. Why? Because today if you go into farming you have to do it on a huge scale, with millions of dollars to put into capital equipment. And you need more special agricultural expertise than has ever been required before because it's more difficult than ever to make a profit in farming.

Slivers of land or unused portions of buildings for billboard sites For me, this has been one of the most profitable places to look for neglected property that has the potential to be turned into a bundle of money.

Sometimes there are wedges of land between different tracts that haven't been consolidated, and those seemingly worthless pieces of property may be more valuable for their size than anything around them. As I said, they could be bought, or more commonly, leased for billboards if the visibility to roadways is good enough. Or they might be sold for high prices to developers who want to put large expanses of land in the area together but can't without the little slivers that exist here and there.

I'll be devoting substantial space later in this book to explain how you can exploit these slivers of real estate to the best advantage. For now, just keep in mind that if you come across one, think twice before you let it slip through your fingers.

Ugly, unattractive real estate adjacent to more attractive, profitable property I'm a great believer in the principle of "value by association"—a variation, I suppose, on "guilt by association." In other words, if you have a booming factory on one lot and a vacant lot next door that looks more like a dump than a piece of prime real estate, you may be looking at the sow's ear that could be turned into the silk purse. I'll show you some ways to do this when we discuss the concept of the "purple tree in the forest" a little later.

Run-down motels, restaurants or other business property It's possible that a business that's being run unsuccessfully on a particular piece of property is a failure because of factors beyond the owner's control—such as poor economic conditions in the area. But more likely the main problem may just be poor management of the business or perhaps the wrong kind of business for the location. If you have a knack for business, always look closely at those that are trying to sell out because you may be able to employ your own business expertise to turn them around—and also turn the property on which they rest into a much more valuable investment.

These, then, are just a few national and local geographical considerations to keep in mind as you look for relatively underpriced property with good growth potential. But even if you know the best places, it's also essential to have a point of view, preferably before you even begin your search and certainly before you put down any money or sign a contract.

3

How to Pick Your
Property Ploy

THE KEY FACTOR in turning depressed or neglected property into a fortune is the basic business idea—or what I call the property ploy.

We've already referred to this concept, but a great deal more remains to be said. The property ploy is the first thing that you should concentrate on as you move seriously into the world of property purchases. In "rags" real estate, as in no other form of investment, it's essential that *before* you buy or lease a tract or building, you must have clearly in mind exactly *how* you want to make money. If you buy first and start thinking afterward about how to turn a profit, the chances are you'll never see a profit.

But how can you come up with a viable property ploy? Or to put it another way, is it possible to *learn* how to formulate a money-making idea that can become the key to turning poor, depressed real estate into a fortune?

I believe it's quite possible to learn how to formulate and put into effect money-making concepts that will result in profits in the thousands and even millions of dollars on undervalued real estate. And to achieve this end, there

43

seem to be at least four major steps in the formulation of an effective property ploy.

Step One: Look for your best ideas in the fields you know best.

This point may seem self-evident, but you'd be amazed at the number of people who try to come up with an idea outside their major fields of expertise. Then, they often devote all sorts of time and money trying to put their idea into effect, only to find in the end that they don't understand the basics of what they are about.

I'm reminded of one guy who knew nothing about the restaurant business, but he saw that a shop had become available on a busy corner in his town, and he decided to buy the building and put up a short-order food stand called Pizzas and Cream. Now I suppose this was a fairly clever *literary* idea, to have a restaurant that was a cute play on the phrase "peaches and cream." But as a real estate and business concept it didn't go anywhere—not because the corner didn't have potential, but because his idea for using the property came from a field he knew nothing about. The long and short of it was that people apparently didn't think it was very appetizing to combine pizzas and ice cream as their fast-food preference, and he soon went out of business.

I've made a number of mistakes in my life as a result of equally bad ideas. But I've also found that my real estate successes have *always* been based on property ploys that have arisen from areas I knew or made a special effort to learn intimately.

For example, advertising, especially through billboards, was one of my early fields of expertise. And predictably, some of my early successes in real estate investment were in the billboard business.

Even when I was a seemingly hopeless drunk, losing one job after another, I discovered that I really liked jobs that involved selling and advertising. Also, I always was too much of a Lone Ranger in business to fit neatly into a bureaucratic organization. So I drifted naturally toward independent jobs that had something to do with advertising. And that meant that after I finally sobered up, I eventually got a job with the Outdoor Advertising Association of America, the national trade association for billboard operators.

One indicator that I was in the right job—an indicator that has always worked for me—was that I had a high level of enthusiasm for my work. For me, being in the right job is like falling in love. You just *know* it when you're in it. If you have a love and an affection for an industry, your level of awareness increases by a couple of hundred percent. Your willingness to stay after five o'clock increases. Your tendency to take your work home with you increases.

As far as I'm concerned, there's nothing more joyful than being in the right job. Joy and happiness at work automatically cause a high level of enthusiasm. And I've never met anyone with a high level of enthusiasm who is not successful. Maybe someday I will meet such a person. But so far, I haven't.

One great thing about a high level of enthusiasm is that it gives you an extra dose of resilience when you fail at a project or goal along the way—and you *will* fail at some point, you can count on that. Also, enthusiasm gives you that perseverance of character that we talked about in the first chapter, that grim determination to keep after a great personal goal until you achieve it.

But perhaps most important of all for our present discussion, high enthusiasm for a given line of work provides the most fertile ground possible for great business ideas— ideas that can become the property ploy that will enable you to turn almost any property, no matter how poor, into a handsome profit.

So I immediately got deeply involved and highly enthusiastic about my job with the trade association for billboard companies. Although I was based in Chicago, my assignment was to travel around the upper Midwest, especially Wisconsin, to prepare billboard operators who were members of our organization for an audit. The main goal was to help them so that they could remain members in good standing of the association.

During these trips, I would "ride" the billboards of each of the operators—in other words, I'd sit in a car next to the owner or his representative, and I'd examine each of his billboards in the area to see if they measured up to our industry standards. My evaluation involved seeing how many feet of wide-open unobstructed visibility the billboard had for motorist traffic. Then, I'd give each billboard a rating: a 10 if it was a maximum value billboard, an 8 if there were some obstructions to clear viewing, and so on.

One of the most important things I learned during these trips was that even though the billboard business was quite profitable, there wasn't a great deal of creativity in the way that most owners operated. The typical billboard operator was very comfortable, fat and complacent. Many of them had other business interests, so that their billboard company was only secondary.

I soon decided there was probably some room for new operators with fresh ideas to enter the market and compete successfully. Sometimes I'd come across such an operator in my travels, and one of these people was a man named Bob Naegele. He was an innovator and competitor in the outdoor advertising business and was quite successful in going up against the big giant of the industry, General Outdoor Advertising.

So I began to study Naegele's approach. I noticed that most other billboard operators used an old-style structure for their posters. They had a wooden frame built relatively close to the ground with green trim and an old latticework design at the bottom. Also, the light fixtures they used were usually three gooseneck incandescent units that hung down off the top of the board and resulted in a rather dull, uneven illumination.

But Naegele had decided to revolutionize this approach. He built his billboards high off the ground, so that he had what we call a good "street impression value." In other words, his boards had a lot of impact on a high percentage of passing traffic. Also, his illumination was far superior to that of his competitors: He used powerful fluorescent fixtures. And for the most part, his structures were built entirely of steel rather than the traditional wood.

Whereas in the past, many billboard operators had a "take it or leave it" attitude toward their advertisers because there had been no choice, now, with Naegele, there *was* a choice, an encouragement for exciting competition. All this made a great impression on me. I saw that Naegele had put together a winning combination, that it was possible to succeed in this business if you had some new ideas and knew the business well. So I decided to become a billboard operator myself and to try out some ideas that had started to germinate in my own mind. These included dramatic things like building the biggest billboard in Wisconsin in an effort to attract more attention than my competitors. I also did some traditional analyses of possible markets so that I could move into areas where there was no effective billboard advertising.

Of course, I had to get financing before I could accomplish any of these tasks, but that's another story. For our present purposes, the important point is that my idea for going into the billboard business—and the special strategies I would use when I did go into that business—came from information I had gathered on my regular job. It's not that I sat down and created a million-dollar business scheme in a whirl of creativity out of whole cloth. On the contrary, I just kept my eyes open at work. And as ideas popped up naturally in the course of my daily tasks, I picked and acted on those concepts and opportunities that seemed most promising.

What was the result of all this?

One result was that I got started in the billboard business, which has become a multimillion-dollar real estate proposition for me around the country. Just to give you an example, some early billboard properties I bought in the very area where I was doing auditing work for the trade association—Terre Haute, Indiana—are still paying off handsomely. I put a little more than $10,000 into these properties between about 1964 and 1977, and they now pay me and my family a steady $4,000 annually in rent income. As you can see, my original capital outlay was paid off long ago, and I continue to get a steady 40 percent return on the initial investment.

But in addition to the billboard opportunities that have opened up for me, I've found that one business involvement always leads to another. Billboards often go up as directional signs for restaurants and motels, and that's been another profitable area of investment for me in recent years, as we'll see in the next chapter.

So remember: Don't go looking in the clouds for your

big money-making concept in depressed real estate. Look in your own backyard!

Step Two: Learn to take a second look.

After you formulate a basic business idea, or property ploy, that you think has the potential to transform depressed or neglected property into an attractive investment, the next step is to start looking around for a tract of land where you can put your idea to work.

But it takes more than just "looking around" for a piece of land. You have to look and then *look again*. This is the essence of what I call my "second-look philosophy." Most people see a piece of real estate that for some reason looks bad, and then they immediately get turned off and start looking elsewhere. It's important, though, not to make up your mind too fast.

Look the property over once, and then turn away if you must. But be sure to grit your teeth and look at least once more. On that second look, try to find positive features to the property you may have overlooked on the first evaluation. Remember: What you're trying to do is find *overlooked* real estate opportunities. So you can assume that you, as well as anyone else, will overlook real bargains if you only check something out once and then move on.

For example, I know some people who might have a negative reaction at first to buying property in northern Florida, in the western strip of land just below Alabama that is known as the Florida panhandle. I was planning to move into there and put together a deal, but one prospective investor kept giving me excuses. He had taken a look

at the area—one look—and had come away with a negative impression that I couldn't change.

I told him, "I think that panhandle area of Florida is
exciting because ground is still very cheap down there.
The tax base is very cheap, very low compared to anywhere else. The people can live there year-round and still
be very comfortable."

"But it gets cold down there in the winter," my friend
said.

"Not as cold as where you live, in New York," I said.

"Yeah, but it's really too hot for me in the summer,
too," he said. "I don't think most people would be interested in that hot-cold combination."

"What else is wrong with the area?" I asked, curious
now about how far his negativism would go.

"Too many bugs."

"Anything else?"

"Florida in general doesn't really have a change of
seasons."

"Too hot, too cold, yet still no change of seasons?" I
asked.

"Right."

"Let me tell you something," I said. "First of all, I don't
think you should invest in this deal I'm putting together
because I don't think you'd ever be comfortable with it.
But I want you to know what I'm really hearing from you.
I'm hearing a personal reaction, not a business judgment.
I'm hearing an automatic kind of negativism, not just a
sound response from a cautious investor. You're burning
a hole in this deal before you've even looked at it very
closely."

In contrast to this fellow, a number of investors I approached did take a second look at the property involved
in one deal I was organizing in northern Florida. And we

made a profit of $400,000 in only eight months. I'll describe this deal in more detail in a later chapter.

But the key lesson I want to get across at this point is that it's absolutely essential that you brace yourself for a bad first reaction when you first evaluate a property that you hope to build into a powerful profit center. That kind of property is, *by definition,* going to look like a white elephant at first. Otherwise, the demand for it would probably be so great that you could never afford to buy it. What you want to do is to search hard for property that appears terrible at first glance but that begins to reveal its true potential when you take a second look at it.

Step Three: Be willing to go through the agony of active risk taking.

Don't ever let anyone fool you about one thing: Making a lot of money in depressed or neglected real estate is never something that promotes a sense of inner peace. Some successful property entrepreneurs may *have* a sense of inner peace, but their tranquillity comes from sources other than their business, such as a firm personal philosophy or religious faith. But that sense of calm and peace won't come from the real estate venture itself—at least not until it's successfully completed!

After you've come up with a good property ploy and found a likely purchase by examining its profit potential thoroughly through the second-look philosophy, then the nerve-racking phase of the deal comes into play: The time has arrived to put yourself and your money on the line. It's at this point that most people drop out of the picture. It's fun to read self-help books on real estate investment.

It's also fun to fantasize about how much money you could make if you did this or that. But when it comes to actually taking some significant risks with their savings or their careers, that gets a little too scary for most people to handle.

And the risks are very real because there really is some reason to be frightened. If you're going to have a chance to make a decent profit on a property investment, it's going to cost some money, no matter how depressed the property is. For most people these days, that means putting most or all of their life savings into a venture that may have a very uncertain future.

Every successful entrepreneur I know has experienced excruciating inner turmoil and anxiety along with his success. Within a year after I had embarked on my own independent real estate ventures, including investments in billboards, I was periodically getting up in the middle of the night and throwing up because I was so worried about how I'd make the next payroll for my three or four employees.

But it's not just the welfare of your workers that worries you. It's also your own family's well-being. Usually, you have to take out a loan from a bank to make up the total investment capital you need for a real estate deal of any type. And in almost every case, the bank will require you to sign the note personally. That means you'll have to agree that if you can't repay the loan, the lender—in most cases, a bank—can come after all your personal assets to satisfy the debt. You could lose your home, everything, if you fail. So there's some reason to be a little nervous about real estate investments of any type.

Now I know I'm painting a rather unpleasant picture here, and you may actually be on the verge of closing this book. But I just want to present an honest evaluation of what you may be getting into if you proceed with any type of real estate concept, including the rags-to-riches approach we're talking about in these pages. There's big money to be made in this approach to property investment, and the risks are often significantly less than in many other types of business ventures. But there are still risks, and unless you prepare carefully and assess all the dangers before you leap, you may find yourself embroiled in more financial trouble than you anticipated.

With careful preparation, however, you can limit your risks and greatly increase your chances to succeed in making a great deal of money out of overlooked property opportunities. It's this positive side of the rags-to-riches approach that I want to emphasize from here on out.

Step Four: Make it happen.

A willingness to take significant risks is an important factor in turning a real estate investment concept into big money. But there is a difference between foolhardy risk taking and the calculated gamble that is required for success. Some people are willing to throw their money away on almost any wild project, and then, more often than not, when the deal falls through—or seems to fall through—they throw up their hands and take their bad fortune as just one of the breaks of life.

But the real winner in rags-to-riches real estate investment first studies the situation and then takes a risk that he believes is reasonable and will result in a good profit. Finally, and perhaps more important, he resolves to stick with the project until it *does* make a profit. It takes a deep, tough commitment to achieve this goal—a commitment that may require long hours of thought and work and probably a few failures before the first big success comes along.

Also, the ability to come up with consistently profitable property ploys depends on your willingness to develop a sense of self-confidence and enthusiasm that you may not now possess but that you *can* possess if you learn to think in terms of setting and believing you can achieve significant long-term goals in the real estate field.

What I'm talking about here is moving beyond the stage of reading and fantasizing about what you would do with a pile of money, if you only had it, and getting into a frame of mind where you've decided that, regardless of the hurdles you must clear, *you are going to make it happen.* Making it happen—that's one of my own personal slogans. And I believe some version of this attitude must become part of the personality of every successful real estate investor.

You can see that here I'm going back to the idea we've already mentioned of developing a property personality —a set of inner traits that will pave the way to success in working with undervalued real estate. I can tell you just so much through a book. At some point you have to incorporate those bits of advice and specific techniques that seem to strike a responsive chord deep within you, and then you have to venture out on your own. Success in this field will come from qualities and desires within you, not from someone leading you by the hand from rags to riches.

Now you have an idea about the steps that are necessary to get to the point of putting together a profitable deal in depressed or overlooked property opportunities. So let's get to the specifics of how to make some money at this game. In the ensuing pages, we'll consider a variety of types of real estate investment that may seem, at first blush, to be total losers. But then we'll "look again," and we'll go into great detail to see exactly how those investments were transformed into fortunes. Finally, we'll consider some general principles that will help you "make it happen" in your own real estate dealings.

4

The Purple Tree
in the Forest

ONE OF THE most important kinds of overlooked or neglected real estate opportunities that I know about is what I call the "purple tree in the forest."

To understand this concept, it's helpful to imagine yourself walking along in a dense, deep-green rain forest, when all of a sudden, you come face to face with this tree that is painted purple. After getting over the shock, you proceed on out of the forest, but as you think back on your walk, what's the main thing you remember? That purple tree, of course.

Your recollections of the tree will probably mostly be negative because it didn't fit into the surrounding natural scenery. But in any case, you'll remember that it was different—and you'll begin to wonder why it was painted that color, who painted it and so forth. That tree will continue to signal to you, call forth your thoughts and ideas. You may even become so obsessed that you decide to try to find out what it's doing there in the midst of all that greenery.

A lot of real estate creates the same impression in the average observer's mind. He looks at a building or a lot, and at first it looks ugly or out of place. The initial reaction may be a combination of revulsion and fascination. But if you find yourself responding that way, don't just drop the matter and go about your business: You may well be in the presence of a "purple tree," and that means you may be looking at a piece of property that may be a big potential profit center *because of* its ugliness or strangeness.

The most obvious example of this sort of phenomenon in real estate is the building or home that seems just a little out of place in the neighborhood where it's located. For example, it may be a run-down house in an upper-income neighborhood. Or it may be an apartment building in a stable or upwardly mobile low-middle-income area that mostly has private homes.

I ran into this last type of property several years ago in Springfield, Illinois. It was a four-family brick apartment-unit building that was in a low- to middle-income residential area. The owner's daughter had just been killed in a freak skating accident, and he was really eager to move out of town and start over again somewhere so that he wouldn't have all the painful memories nagging away at him.

But even though he advertised the building for several weeks in the local newspaper, there were no takers. I learned later that a number of people had inquired after seeing the ad. But they decided, "No, that building is in a bad neighborhood." Or, "No, that's almost exclusively a single-family-house area. That building just doesn't fit in."

But they failed to take a second look and see that the very fact that the neighborhood was in the low- to middle-income range meant that there was plenty of room for reasonably priced apartments. Some people at that income level simply couldn't afford to buy a home until they built up a little capital, and an apartment was just the thing for them until they were prepared to purchase their own home.

Also, I learned after looking the place over and talking to the present tenants that the families who were living in the building had been there a long time. The landlord didn't have to worry about frequent turnovers and periods of vacancy while he was trying to locate another tenant.

So when the man offered me the building for $60,000, I immediately accepted. Not only was the price a bargain, but also the terms were extremely attractive. I didn't have to put any money down; I just had to assume a first and second mortgage. The first was held by a savings and loan association, and the second, for $10,000, was held by the seller. And because he had advance rent deposits from his tenants that he credited to me, I didn't have to pay anything in the way of fees at the time we closed the deal.

Three years later, I sold the apartment building for $78,000—an $18,000 profit in only three years. And all I had put into the property, aside from normal maintenance, were my monthly mortgage payments. During those three years, I also had the benefit of a regular income stream from the apartment rentals—income that was sheltered from taxes by write-offs for depreciation and other deductions.

So even though this apartment building may have seemed an out-of-place "purple tree in the forest," it turned into a very *profitable* "tree" without my doing anything unusual to enhance its value. I just kept it up, sat on it as surrounding real estate values rose, and then sold painlessly at a profit when I got good and ready. So to sum up, the seller was paid his asking price, but in exchange he gave me good terms in financing the sale and thus provided an excellent incentive for me to buy.

* * *

Even though it didn't take much effort for me to make a good profit on this piece of overlooked property, it usually takes a great deal of thought and work—especially if your goal is to make not just a nice, moderate profit but a fortune.

That was the situation I faced with the Hen House restaurant chain I built in the Midwest—in Indiana, Illinois and Missouri. This is one of the best examples I can imagine of a profitable "purple tree," because with some of the ugliest, most unwanted property imaginable and an initial investment of only $15,000, I ended up as the majority stockholder in a restaurant chain worth about $10 million.

Here's the way my fellow investors and I "made it happen" in that situation.

First of all, the basic idea—or what we've come to know as a property ploy—for the eventual restaurant chain arose from my own broad expertise in a field I knew well, the billboard business. I had a billboard company in Springfield, Illinois, and like most billboard businesses, there was advertising space that wasn't rented out all year long.

My business was typical of many billboard companies, with the space rented out about 85 percent of the time, or the equivalent each year of about two months worth of unsold advertising space. Since I could make about $40,000 a month when I was operating at full capacity, the two months of vacancies meant I was missing about $80,000 a year in income. So I began looking for ways to decrease the amount of vacant space and increase my cash flow.

It struck me, as I pondered my billboard dilemma, that if I had other business interests and could *trade* my vacant space for advertising my other interests in another medium, I would be much better off than just allowing my boards to sit unsold. So I began to toy with an idea that had long fascinated me—the restaurant business.

I knew nothing about establishing and running a restaurant. But at the same time, I knew that restaurants are, at their foundation, a real estate enterprise. You have to have a tract of land, a building and the business concept for the restaurant that will allow you to turn your investment into a profit. I realized that if I had some restaurants in my investment portfolio, I would be able to approach some of the local Illinois television stations: I could propose that I would give them space on my vacant billboards if they would give me an equal amount of value on the air in commercial advertising time.

There were several advantages to this idea. First of all, by diversifying my real estate investments in this way, I would expand my personal real estate expertise. I could also protect myself by spreading my risks through an unrelated property investment (the restaurant business) in case of possible bad times in the billboard business. Finally, getting into the restaurant business seemed to offer the potential of making my billboard enterprise even more lucrative by reducing the vacant advertising space.

So I decided to test the waters with several TV stations, and, sure enough, they were interested. As a result, I worked out a deal with a couple of them who were willing to swap their time for billboard exposure. Then, I began to look around for a restaurant.

Now, you see what's happened here so far: I came up with a money-making idea out of my own field of expertise (even though any final restaurant deal would have to involve my learning a great deal more about that business and also finding people with special skills in this field who could help me "make it happen"). Then, I immediately went into action to try to put a deal together.

Of course, I had a long, complex way to go before my

property ploy became a profit-making reality: The main difficulty was that I was trying to combine *two* property ploys—one to enhance the value of my billboards, and another to establish a successful restaurant or restaurant chain. The first idea was on the verge of becoming reality, but it depended on the success of the second. And the second, the building of a viable restaurant business, was a long way from fruition.

So I immediately set out to see what I could do to understand the restaurant business and establish myself as a successful real estate entrepreneur in that field. I formed a company called Cardinal Industries with about ten other investors, and we began to search for a going restaurant business that we could buy.

It was at this point that my rags-to-riches orientation toward real estate came into play. I wanted to find a business that had plenty of potential, but one that also was undervalued because it had some sort of trouble or image that I felt I could correct.

The first idea we considered was a barbecue franchise in St. Louis, but our negotiations with the owner went nowhere and eventually the deal fell through. Some tremendous good came out of those talks, however, because one of the officers in the barbecue company was working on an idea that eventually made him, me and a number of other people a great deal of money.

He told me about this concept he had to establish a chain of small restaurants, with maybe twenty seats each, alongside existing gasoline stations on major highways. Now here was something that interested me. Almost immediately, I could see that we were looking at a purple tree in the forest. The land next to most highway filling stations was usually the ugliest, most unattractive you could imagine. Typically, the tracts would be barren of trees and shrubbery, and more often than not there were pieces of junk littered here and there. And over the whole scene hung the unpleasant odor of car exhaust and other filling-station fragrances.

It was easy to write off these adjoining tracts as useless for anything. But after a second look at these "purple trees," all sorts of money-making ideas came to mind— not the least of which was the restaurant concept. The interstate highways had very few "feeding systems" at that time. And those that were available didn't offer a continuous standard of high quality that a good chain could.

The kind of restaurant that my business acquaintance had in mind would specialize in breakfasts, mainly because that's the highest-profit item in the restaurant business. I thought his idea had real possibilities, in part because the restaurant would be guaranteed a regular stream of traffic because of the gas station. Also, the land next to the existing stations would probably be cheap to lease. In many cases, the gas station owner's adjacent properties were going to waste, so many would probably jump at the chance to get at least *some* additional income from their real estate.

But even though this seemed a property ploy with great potential, the idea was just on the verge of being stillborn. My friend had no money, and I was reluctant to commit myself because I wasn't crazy about some of his associates. So he finally decided to move ahead without me: He borrowed about $40,000 and made some effort to get a restaurant going. But he went broke within a few months without ever breaking ground for a building.

Still, though, this man and his partners didn't drop the idea. They continued to play with it, and before long, I was talking with them again. I told them that even though they had a feasible concept, they didn't have a clear idea of where their company was headed.

"Why didn't you go ahead and start building a restaurant when you had some money?" I asked.

"Because if we built one, we'd have to tell people what it earns, and if it turns out it loses money rather than makes a profit, that would destroy our idea," one of them told me.

"What exactly *is* your idea?" I asked.

"We've decided we want to promote the restaurant idea as a franchise called 'Hen House.' And we've been talking to Jimmy Dean about promoting the idea for us."

I could see immediately what they were trying to do. They just wanted to come up with what looked like a good franchise idea on paper without ever testing it out in an actual restaurant situation. Then, they would sell the idea to a celebrity like Dean and go around collecting front-end money from the public by selling franchises. If the franchise system made it, that would be well and good. But if the franchises bombed, they could just walk away with the money they had taken up front.

This idea struck me as being one that was going nowhere. It was a thinly veiled get-rich-quick scheme that depended more on selling an untested idea to the public and to Jimmy Dean than on a solid business foundation that would have some chance of long-term success. It's not that I have anything against making a lot of money in a short period of time. On the contrary, I *like* doing business that way. But I believe there has to be something more substantive than sleight of hand in any legitimate real estate venture.

So I went ahead and continued negotiating with these guys, but I made it clear I wouldn't go along with their franchise plan. And as a matter of fact, I met Jimmy Dean soon after these conversations and told him straight out that I didn't think our restaurant idea was far enough along for him to get involved.

By this time I was reaching the point that I had to fish or cut bait with this Hen House group. They had a lot of things going against them. First of all, they didn't have enough money to proceed any further. And also, they were a body without a head. There was no real leadership, and all their dealings with one another were characterized by conflict and confusion. I failed to find one key guy who could say, "Hey, tomorrow morning, everybody show up at eight o'clock!"—and expect to have anyone follow him.

But they also had some important strengths. I felt their idea was basically sound, and they had done some meaningful planning, such as drawing up a good set of menus. Also, many of the people who had tied up their money in the scheme seemed like decent folks, and most of them knew more about the restaurant business than I did.

More than once, I was on the verge of walking away from them and trying another approach on my own. But finally, I decided they had more going for than against them, and so I made them an offer.

"I'll buy into your company only if I can buy certain shareholders out," I said. There were several disaffected people who I knew would do more harm than good if they stayed with us, and so I wanted to terminate their employment as soon as possible.

"Also, all the money I invest has to go into working capital—and that means that we build one restaurant to see what we've really got in this Hen House concept of yours." I wasn't about to put my money into a bottomless pit that would go to pay off their debts and never contribute to giving their basically good idea a fighting chance.

Finally, I told them, "I'll put seventy-five thousand dollars into your company on behalf of my group, Cardinal Industries, but in return we want a majority interest in the company."

As I had anticipated, they accepted my offer, and my fellow Cardinal Industries investors and I ended up with about 60 percent of the company's stock, which gave us total control of the company. Over the years that we built the business up, I took company shares instead of a salary until I have now ended up with about 55 percent of the outstanding shares of the corporation. Most of these shares came to me because I personally took some risks and gave guarantees to banks for working capital and restaurant equipment financing.

Now that we had set up our deal, the time had arrived to make it happen. I knew that the first thing we had to do was do our homework so that we would be in a strong position to go to some gas station owner and sell him on our idea. This meant, first of all, getting all the financial details and projections together into some understandable form. Also, we had to make some final decisions about precisely what the food and decor for our restaurant would be like.

Now, to understand exactly how a deal like this is put together, let's consider each of these factors in turn.

1. The financial branch of our purple tree. To sell a property ploy to anybody, you've got to have your numbers straight. You have to know your business forward and backward. Your prospective purchaser doesn't want to have to do your homework for you. He doesn't want to be your banker and your custodian—your mother, father, husband or wife.

So we figured out exactly what it would cost for us to put up a building on a gas station site. This included such costs as those for restaurant personnel, food and building maintenance. By our calculations, back in the late 1960s when we got started, we were going to have to make enough to cover expenses of $2,400 a week just to break even.

Then, we sat down to try to project *realistically* what our income might be from a typical restaurant attached to a gas station. The first thing we wanted to do was to try to determine the number of customers we could expect. And the best way to do this seemed to be to make a projection based on the number of gallons of gasoline pumped annually at a given location. So if a typical location put out 600,000 gallons a year, with the average car filling up with about ten gallons, then we could expect 60,000 cars to come across the property (600,000 divided by 10 equals 60,000).

Next, we worked out the average number of people in each car on the highway—say about 3.2—and then calculated that the total number of people the normal gas station was servicing was about 192,000 people (3.2 times 60,000 equals 192,000). Finally, we decided that we would shoot for 60 percent of these gas station customers, or about 115,200 people each year as our restaurant customers. If our customers had an average food purchase of $1.30 per person, that would mean a gross annual restaurant income of nearly $150,000, or almost $2,900 a week —an income that would be comfortably higher than the $2,400 a week we had figured we needed to survive.

I should mention before we proceed any further that these were conservative estimates we were making about our potential income. For example, the estimate for average check charges for each of our customers was based on a 30 percent food cost. But in reality, breakfast food costs were only about 20 percent of the menu prices, and lunch items were around 30 to 35 percent. Since we planned to concentrate on a breakfast menu served at all hours, we could count on a higher profit.

Also, the estimate of the number of customers we might attract didn't include the people who *lived* near the restaurant. If you took an airplane ride around a ten-mile radius of any of the Hen House sites we were consid-ering, you'd see there might be 25,000 people scattered around in the homes in the area.

Now, think about it: How would you like to own the only restaurant in a town of 25,000? That was in fact what we had a chance to achieve with our Hen House concept.

To do well with a brand-new restaurant on a highway, it always helps to attract *repeat* local customers. The best way to achieve this is to serve high-quality food at low prices. For us, the local people would become a backup to our tourist-traveler income. If we became too tourist-oriented, we might alienate the locals and end up with only a five-month instead of a ten-month cash flow.

2. The food branch of the purple tree. As I've said, we had decided to concentrate on a breakfast menu in our restaurant, not only because it had the highest profit mar-gin, but also, in the words of one of the restaurant experts I got to know, because it was "one of the hardest meals to foul up!" In other words, bacon and eggs is a hard dish to cook really poorly, and it's normally one of the cheapest things on most menus. So travelers are more likely to choose a dish like this rather than something more com-plicated—including an item as common as a hamburger.

I suppose the main problem that most prospective restaurant patrons have is that initially they don't trust a new restaurant and especially ones on the highway. They assume you're going to give them something bad to medi-ocre, and they're pleasantly surprised when you give them a meal of superior quality. So what we had to do was to identify the type of food our traveling patrons were most likely to order first. Then, when they began to trust us and to associate quality with the Hen House name, they would come back and order something more complicated and expensive.

So we decided that when a person ordered eggs and

bacon or sausage, we'd give him the works. We would use a big, oval plate with a full meal heaped on it. Although we planned to "portion control" the food closely to keep a handle on our costs, we decided to include a couple of eggs, a healthy portion of bacon or sausage, some home fries and good biscuits on a separate plate with some fresh jams, jellies and butter. In addition, we served the best coffee money could buy, along with free refills.

We expected our typical customer to be pleasantly surprised with this kind of presentation because he would get more than he expected. And he would be *doubly* surprised later on when he got his bill and saw the low cost for the amount of food he had consumed. By building confidence in one lead item this way, we hoped to develop a customer who would come back later on, either at this restaurant or another Hen House down the road.

At this point, you may be asking, "What does all this restaurant lore have to do with real estate investment?" But remember: Right now, we're talking about part of the property ploy, the business idea that we had settled upon to turn that vacant, unattractive land near highway gas stations into a profit center. In every case, to turn a piece of "rags" real estate into real riches, you have to combine a promising business concept with your neglected or depressed property, and that's the process we're going through right now.

This is not a fly-by-night, easy-money kind of scheme I'm talking about. No successful real estate project is. You may make a fortune quickly, but to make even a small profit, not to mention really big money, takes a lot of thought and planning. The "numbers" and, in this particular case, the menus of the Hen House concept were extremely important—but no more important than the decor and the type of building we would erect next to those gas stations.

3. The building branch of the purple tree. I had a
definite idea about what I wanted the Hen House restaurants to look and "feel" like, but I ran into a lot of opposi-
tion from some of my new partners on this score. It's
purely a personal thing with me, but I didn't want anything to do with those restaurants where you have to wait
in lines and go up and down aisles. They strike me as
being like the food lines in a prison—and remember, I
spent more time than I like to think about in jails before
I stopped drinking.

I think it's essential to have some personal contact the
moment you walk into a restaurant, to have a hostess or
waitress greet you. Somebody who has been driving hundreds of miles down a highway with his or her family
needs a comfortable place to sit down at a table and be
waited on. These people are tired, and they don't want to
make a lot of decisions about how to put their own cafete-
ria menu together. Also, they want the decor to be warm
and familylike and not be so sterile that it looks like it's
been hosed down every night.

So after consulting with my wife Ellie, who has had
some experience in interior decoration, I came up with
some proposals that were consistent with these ideas of
warmth and comfort.

Specifically, we selected a "predated" design for the
building—a rustic sort of look that we felt would never go
out of style. We didn't want to be constantly going
through the hassle of redecorating and changing the place
to keep up with new design trends. Also, we decided that
a building designed somewhat like a real hen house would
be compatible with our basic theme and also with a "rural
eating" concept.

Inside the building, we decided to put oil lamps, farm
implements and other curiosities that you could pick up
at local farm auctions. With these little artifacts hanging

around on the walls, we found we got people interested in the atmosphere as well as the food. I still often hear our guests ask a waitress, "Hey, what was that thing used for?"

Ellie would travel out to garage and barn sales in central Illinois and purchase all sorts of unique items for as little as fifty cents each. She also arranged to electrify old oil lamps for our table lighting. The customer comment cards consistently raved about the decorating—again, it was the *concept,* not the expense.

The physical approach I wanted to take was fine with my Cardinal Industries group of original investors, but several of my new partners weren't impressed. They were more concerned with traffic. "Move 'em in, and move 'em out!" they said.

The problem was that they didn't understand *people* traffic. It was almost as though they were prepared to treat people like automobiles. They didn't understand what motivates people to come back to a place. They also were concerned about making a good, high-traffic impression for a while with this one place so that we could use it as a model to sell a bunch of franchises and also sell stock to the public.

I finally had to lay it on the line with them. "Baby," I said, "it's our dough, and we're going to do it our way. If we're going to have a loss, it will be our money going down the tubes. Furthermore, we're not going to sell any franchises in this company. And we're certainly not going to go public or talk to any stockbrokers until we build our first Hen House and find out if we've got a loser or not. If we've got a loser, we'll take it on the chin and go home. If all the homework we've done, all the testing and planning and converting traffic to guest checks doesn't work, then we've lost. I'd rather have one loser than ten, even if those ten are franchises."

A few of the guys still disagreed with me, and they

eventually fell by the wayside; and I bought their shares as they pulled out because I was sure we were on the right track.

But even though we had altered the menus and the design of the restaurant from what the original people had first envisioned, we never lost sight of the key original idea—to hook up our restaurant with an existing gas station. We knew in general the kind of purple tree we had to find. But our next task was to find the specific one that seemed to have the most potential for what we were trying to accomplish with our particular property ploy.

So we began to talk up our Hen House idea with several station owners who had likely sites, and eventually we came in contact with a fellow who was a Standard Oil of Indiana dealer in Gardner, Illinois. Our basic pitch to him was: "If we put food next door to your gasoline station, you could offer one-stop shopping to the people on the highway, and you'd be in a stronger position to sell more gas."

When you're trying to make a real estate deal "happen," and your property ploy involves selling to a businessman, the strongest point you can make will center on how your product or service can help the guy do his job better. And for this gas station owner, "better" meant faster, more efficiently or more profitably.

Our idea really appealed to him because in trying to sell our real estate concept we appealed to his main interest, which was selling gasoline. We showed him that offering food would naturally increase the number of cars pulling up to his gas pumps. Also, we weren't talking about a huge capital investment on his part. He was leasing the land, and we wanted to sublet a plot from him for twenty years.

Eventually, after the restaurant had been going for a while, we bought the building from the owner. The building, by the way, was of modular wood construction and could be relocated if the operation failed. This precaution took some of the edge off the risk of construction costs.

The station owner also agreed to put up the money to build the forty-two-seat restaurant building and to blacktop the property alongside his gas station for a driveway and parking for the facility. His end of the capital outlay came to about $60,000. He was also to be responsible for any "extraordinary maintenance," for such things as air-conditioning and replacement of damaged utilities.

For our part, we agreed to put in the restaurant equipment, which ran about $30,000 for pots, pans, grills, vents and a fire extinguisher system. We also told him we would pay him 5 percent of our food sales in excess of $50,000 a year, and by our conservative projections that promised to bring him about $7,500 annually. Also, we guaranteed to reimburse him each year for 12 percent of his total initial cost of about $60,000, or a payment of about $7,200 annually.

This relationship that we settled on turned out to be a very good real estate marriage, but not just because of the clauses in the contract we finally signed. I could tell after a couple of meetings with this owner that he was just right for what we were trying to do with the "purple tree" property next to his station. He was a bit of a promoter type, with enough of a desire to increase his gas sales that he was willing to take a chance on us. He was as motivated to sell gas as we were to sell food—and that was a key trait we needed to make this rags-to-riches concept work. Also, he was as impressed by our enthusiastic 100 percent interest in selling food as we were by his enthusiastic 100 percent interest in selling gas and being a fair landlord.

He took a big gamble on us inasmuch as we were a brand-new company that hadn't even built one building yet. But he sensed, as we did, that you could make almost any decent property ploy happen if you had enough enthusiasm. He knew instinctively that his gas sales would go up if he could get the right kind of people to build a restaurant next to him. So it was natural that we finally came to a mutual understanding and put up our first Hen House on his property.

We proceeded with construction of the restaurant, and everything went smoothly until we tried to get a $40,000 loan from a bank for the equipment package. They refused to give us the money unless it was personally guaranteed. That meant that one or more of the investors had to agree to make themselves and their personal assets liable for payment of the debt if any of the regular monthly payments were missed.

I sent out a letter to every one of our shareholders in the company offering two shares of stock for every dollar's worth of financing they would guarantee. To be entirely fair to them, I must admit this wasn't a very good deal. The stock at that time wasn't worth ten cents on the dollar, and we didn't have even a dime of income at that stage. As a result, there were no takers, and so I had to guarantee a $40,000 loan by myself. In return, I was able to acquire an extra 80,000 shares of stock.

The loan was made to Hen House by the First National Bank of Springfield in Springfield, Illinois. To this day, we still continue to do business with that bank because they had the courage and faith that we needed as a fledgling business. Although we have been approached by larger banks, I have refused to change from this excellent institution. At times, this bank has been somewhat conservative in our dealings with them, but that has also proved to be one reason for our success. Oftentimes, a conservative banker will force you to "do your homework," and as a result, errors in your planning frequently surface before it's too late.

With all our planning, building and financing in place, we finally opened for business, and during our first year of operation, we hit our income projections on the nose, almost to the penny. We brought in an average income of nearly $3,000 a week, more than enough to cover our basic expenses and make a respectable profit—a profit that was sheltered from taxes through the depreciation deductions and other tax breaks we were able to take advantage of as a real estate investment.

Also, our gasoline partner's sales shot up, and his percentage of our food sales and his other income sources from the restaurant operation provided him with a substantial increase in his income.

This first taste of success was just the beginning. Even though I had insisted on establishing a solid, small-scale test of our restaurant concept on that unattractive, "purple-tree" land next to a gas station, my ultimate ambitions were much more expansive. I've found that a successful rags-to-riches real estate venture is usually a step-by-step process:

You first lay a strong foundation just to see if your idea is viable in the marketplace. If it's not, you immediately cut your losses, fold up shop and try something else. In any case, if you do fail—and I have fallen short myself on a number of occasions—then you stand to lose less with an operation that is small and has a minimum amount of money invested at the beginning than you do with an overextended financial commitment.

On the other hand, if your small-scale test proves to be successful, then you should be prepared to move quickly to expand it as much as you reasonably can. If you don't act to get as much mileage as fast as you can out of a good idea, someone else will see what you've done and beat you to it.

Perhaps most important of all, the time has finally

come to think big at this stage of the development of your business. You have to think small at first just to see what kind of an idea you've got. But when you know you have a winner, don't hold back! Be prepared to deal with the biggest corporations if necessary to expand your property ploy to its full potential. And don't allow them to talk you into a deal that will give you less than your success shows you're worth.

As it happened, Standard Oil of Indiana got wind of our success. They were impressed by the increase in gasoline sales at the station in Gardner, and so they asked me to come to Chicago to meet their people in the "new business," or capital investments, department. When I walked into their offices, I was all prepared to take our idea full-scale with them if they could give us a contract with attractive terms.

"Hey, have you got any real estate on the interstate highways that's not developed?" I asked them, almost before we had gotten seated. "I'd like to enter into a deal with you, and I think if we can get our heads together, we can both make a lot of money."

It may be that I came on a little too strong with them. I was an entrepreneur who was just coming off a significant success, and I was excited and enthusiastic because I *knew* a deal could be set up with Standard Oil that would be beneficial to both of us. But I forgot temporarily that they weren't entrepreneurs: They were corporate employees who didn't have their own money on the line—or, as we say, they didn't have any "blood in the deal." They had also been conditioned to think in terms of conservatism and caution when looking for places to put the company's money.

But in any case, I barged on ahead and told them exactly what was on my mind. I said, "These elaborate, Williamsburg-type buildings you put up on the highways aren't the best use of your money. You're spending a load of dough on exotic pump islands, when our experience shows that most people who stop for gas want to get fed at the same time. The problem is that you're not meeting that need.

"What I can offer you is a good feeding system with our Hen House restaurants. I'd like to go out on these properties you have in your soil bank, these unused tracts adjacent to your gas stations, and put up some Hen Houses and make a lot of money for both of us."

As we talked, I agreed to expand our original idea so that I would arrange to have the gasoline pumped as well. I said I'd build a structure alongside my restaurant to accommodate my pump island personnel. But I also said I would want to get rid of the "back room" stuff in the stations—the tires, batteries, and accessories that seemed to me to be so unnecessary on an interstate highway because they weren't sold in a sufficiently high volume. I felt that in light of the few times that those items were bought, they did not provide much of a return on capital investment.

All that I wanted Standard Oil to do was put their marketing equipment in, including the tanks in the ground, the pump islands, the pumping mechanisms and a canopy over the facilities. Also, they would have to pay for the blacktopping that was necessary for the pump islands and other gasoline services.

For my part, I told them I'd buy the Hen House building. But, I said, "I need your ground. You'll have to subordinate your ground in order for me to get my financing at a bank." In other words, they would have to pledge their ground to guarantee my mortgage if I borrowed money from a bank for my buildings.

Also, because our building was a modular type, I impressed Standard Oil with the fact that they would not have to remain in the restaurant business if I failed. The building could be easily removed, and they could convert to a conventional station in the event we were unsuccessful. In this way, we tried to anticipate some of the objections they were likely to make even before they raised them.

Even though our discussions were moving along in a calm, rational fashion, it soon became apparent that they thought I was crazy. They weren't about to go along with most of my ideas, even though I could show they were perfectly sound. Why? For one thing, they didn't completely understand what I was talking about, and they were afraid of taking a risk on something that wasn't thoroughly clear to them. Also, they were conservative businessmen who believed in testing the waters *very* carefully, first only with the tip of the big toe before they even considered sticking their feet in.

But they were obviously impressed enough by the Hen House concept to be unwilling to kick me out the door without some sort of counteroffer. As a result, they suggested that our company take over the management of their Farmer's Table system of restaurants and gasoline services in the Midwest.

Although I knew I didn't want to get involved with those restaurants, I was at least encouraged by their willingness to continue our talks. So I proceeded to show them why the Farmer's Table system was much less attractive than our Hen House concept.

Standard Oil had estimated that start-up costs for one Farmer's Table operation were about $400,000 to $500,000, and this amount didn't include the outlays for gasoline marketing equipment. In contrast, our Hen House buildings, not including the ground costs, ran about $60,000, and the equipment for the restaurants, including furniture, was another $30,000 to $40,000 at the most. So we could go into business with a Hen House restaurant for only about $100,000, while it took about $500,000 for their Farmer's Table approach.

I also felt the locations for the Farmer's Table restaurants weren't good, and Standard Oil required too many percentages and fees for our management of them to be worthwhile. Finally, by merely being managers of their already-existing system, we would be more under their control and would have to go along with whatever they wanted us to do.

As far as we were concerned, it was a deal with Hen House or nothing, and the oil company was impressed enough by our performance to proceed with the negotiations on that basis. In other words, despite the pressure they had put on us, we stuck to our original property ploy because we knew it worked. And our firm resolve not to budge from our basic idea was a major factor that eventually made us a fortune.

But this is not to say that we didn't bend and compromise plenty before we finally got them to sign on the dotted line. As a matter of fact, we gave in much more than I preferred. But I knew if we could get at least one profitable deal going with them, we would be in a position to set up many more, either with Standard or with other oil companies.

So we agreed to do things we really didn't want to do: We bore half the cost of the septic system, offered green stamps, accepted a site that was completely hidden from the major highway and made other concessions until finally we had a deal with them. Their investment at the site came to a total of $40,000, and in return they were to receive from us as a form of rent more than a penny per gallon on gas we sold and also 5 percent of our food sales in excess of $50,000.

Then with the deal in our pocket, we went to work to

show our Hen House concept could be profitable even under adverse conditions.

The only visibility we had was an 80-foot high-rise sign that Standard had put up. They figured that our station would pump about 300,000 gallons that year, considering the fact that we were in an out-of-the-way place and were close to several other competing stations.

But they were wrong. In our first year our station pumped 900,000 gallons of gasoline—three times what they had projected. And our Hen House restaurant hit $200,000 in food sales, a figure far above what we needed to turn a respectable profit. Also, because Hen House was responsible for the gasoline as well as food sales, we were able to enhance our profitability still further by amortizing our costs of operation between both the gasoline and food sales.

To put our success in the terms that a major oil company uses, we had an amazing return on investment. On their $40,000 investment, Standard got a $7,500 profit from our food sales, more than $9,000 in rent and an enormous profit in the extra volume of gasoline we sold. When they compared that with the $700,000 or more that they had invested in sites with lower sales, fifteen miles on either side of us, they were soon knocking on our doors to get us to dig a hole for their Hen House location number two.

But now *we* had the "full house," and I was fully prepared to do the dealing. They called us back to Chicago for more meetings on additional restaurants, and like seemingly dutiful lackeys, a couple of my Hen House partners and I entered their offices, hats in hand.

"Okay, we think just maybe you have a chance," one of their top people told me. "Maybe you can make it after all. Now look, we have these other three properties over here." And he pointed to a map. "We've decided to let you try again on one of these and see if you were just lucky the first time. Of course, the terms and conditions will be the same as before."

"No, no, no," I said. "No, no, no. It's a different ball game now. An entirely different game. That first deal we did with you was just sales promotion—to show you what we could do under the worst conditions. From now on, *we're* going to deal—a brand-new deal."

They almost dropped dead in their tracks. But we didn't even make them a counterproposal. We just told them to make the next deal much sweeter than the first, and we walked away.

Maybe we shouldn't have been quite so confident. I wouldn't advise you to be that cocky because you could alienate a possible corporate partner who could give you a deal that would make you comfortable for the rest of your life. But that was just my personality, to be a little cocky and rub their noses in our success a little bit.

We were buoyed by the success of our first two Hen Houses, and we were confident now that we could make the concept work anywhere there was a decent gas station location—or raw, unused ground near the pumping facilities. We had already started conversations with the Sun Oil Company and a distributor of theirs with whom we got along real well: That was part of the reason for our confidence. Sun was willing to build our Hen House buildings, lease them back to us and then give us the gasoline business along with the restaurants. We started breaking ground on those sites immediately, and the locations became profitable almost as soon as the doors were opened. And they're still profitable today.

Before long, Standard Oil also got back in touch with us, singing a much sweeter tune than they had before.

Today, there are twenty-eight Hen House restaurants in Illinois, Indiana, and Missouri, and we've expanded the capacity to eighty-four seats. As I've already mentioned, my initial personal investment in the company was $15,000 back in 1968, and through the years I've purchased extra shares from the other shareholders and provided them with large capital gains. One of the main reasons for my accumulation of these additional shares is that I continued to guarantee loans, land leases and equipment financing. The same opportunity for stock ownership was always given to other shareholders of the company as well as to the officers, but only a few agreed to accept stock for such personal exposure. A recent valuation of the entire business placed the company's worth at about $10 million. Between my personal investments and a trust set up for my children, I now hold 55 percent of the company's stock.

Not a bad growth record for a "purple tree."

I've spent this much time discussing the Hen House concept just to give you an idea of how much time, thought and effort it can take to turn a "purple tree in the forest" into a fortune. Despite the many uncertainties and personal risks, the entire experience was exhilarating and tremendous fun for me because I love to put deals like this together. But to succeed in something like this, you have to be willing to stick with it, probably over a period of several years.

As we've seen, the basic concept, or property ploy, was really quite simple. The beginnings of the idea of acquiring real estate to set up a restaurant came from a need I had to make my billboard business more profitable by cutting down on vacant advertising space. So I came up with an idea to start a restaurant and exchange advertising opportunities with local television and radio stations.

Then, my restaurant idea was expanded and became more specific when the partners I hooked up with in the original Hen House group contributed their concept of using vacant land near highway gas station sites. This idea became firm as we all took a "second look" at those sites and saw that it was, indeed, quite likely that despite their ugliness and the fact that they had been neglected for years they had the potential to be quite profitable. Every raw, two-acre site became a potential target because we knew how much money could be made from the combination of gasoline, food and gift shop sales.

But there were many twists and turns, wheelings and dealings, before we finally succeeded in setting up the first and the second Hen Houses. After that, of course, our property ploy and "purple tree" combined to produce a fortune for us in short order.

It's important for you to realize, however, that there will probably never be another Hen House chain. There will certainly be many more successful restaurant ideas that can turn poor property into a great deal of money. But the convergence of specific factors that worked for us in the Midwest will probably never happen quite that way again.

So it may be instructive to study our experience and see how the various basic principles of rags-to-riches real estate can work in a concrete situation. But don't use it as a mechanical blueprint for your own concept. Your experience will be unique, as ours was.

If you (1) formulate a good idea, (2) test it carefully, (3) find an undervalued "purple-tree" piece of property that goes with your property ploy, then (4) *stick with it,* you'll *make it happen!* Making money in neglected and overlooked real estate is really rather easy if you plan your strategy well and then have the character to persevere until you succeed.

5

The Bargain Basement of the Real Estate Business

MANY OF THE DEALS that I discuss in this book are illustrated by personal experiences that I have had in the real estate market. Sometimes the transactions may seem to involve monumental amounts of money—or certainly far more capital than you may feel you have to invest.

But it's important not to be intimidated by big figures. The principles that we're discussing apply to *any* property deal, no matter how large or small. Business real estate, which you can turn into a fortune, is often available at the same price—and often even at a lower price—than what it costs to buy a home. It's just a matter of shopping around and, perhaps most important of all, knowing what kinds of cheap real estate to look for.

Even though all of the principles discussed in this book can be used by the small real estate entrepreneur, some of the opportunities may be more difficult to find than others in certain parts of the country if your financing is severely limited. So in this chapter, I want to focus on a few property ploys that are *especially* suitable for the small investor and probably would be readily available almost anywhere you look.

Before we say one more word about this topic, however, let me reiterate a key point I've made elsewhere: No matter how much money you've got, it's a mistake in the current economy to put your available capital into a home and expect to increase the size of your estate by any significant amount.

Those who rely on home ownership to multiply their wealth are victims of what I call the "feudal-manor mentality." There is a myth that exists in the minds of many people that in order to be a "substantial person" or a "man (or woman) of means" it's necessary to own a home.

Now, I happen to own a home myself. But I don't count on that home ownership to be a significant part of my investments. In fact, I don't regard that home as an investment at all. I may very well be able to sell it at some point in the future at a reasonable or even substantial profit. But I can make much more by taking my free capital assets and concentrating them on property that can be exploited through a *business* rather than residential concept.

So you'll find, as we move through this particular discussion, that my main concern is with "small-potatoes" business real estate and not with residential property. Also, in accordance with most of the advice I have to give, these ideas and illustrations are intended primarily to stimulate you to come up with special approaches of your own, not to provide blueprints for precise ways that you can make a million in the rags-to-riches real estate business.

Now, with these preliminaries out of the way, let's get down to some specifics.

One of the best ideas I've come across in my own real estate dealings is the "bed-and-breakfast" approach to offering traveling motorists decent, homey accommodations. This idea is quite popular in England, Ireland and various sections of continental Europe. But it seems to have been tried only on a small scale in this country, and there appears to be plenty of room for the right person with just the right touch to make a real killing.

In case you're unaware of what the bread-and-breakfast system is all about, let me explain briefly. The main idea is to provide travelers with a clean but very simple place to sleep and also to throw a nice breakfast into the cost of the room. But when I say "simple," I don't mean sparsely furnished or sterilely designed. In fact, one of the main attractions of the bed-and-breakfast concept is that the average tourist and business traveler is drawn to the homelike atmosphere these places have to offer, especially if they are modeled after those in many parts of England and Ireland.

There, nice, warm, wooden furniture and bright-colored throw rugs and bedspreads often give you the impression that you are visiting in the home of a friend rather than paying an innkeeper. And when you go downstairs to eat breakfast in the morning, more often than not you're served platters of home-made biscuits, eggs in the style of your choice and sausages or bacon—all on tables with linen tablecloths in a dining room that resembles something your grandmother might have had.

The actual furnishings in these places are not at all expensive. They may be bought at auction sales or other secondhand outlets. But most people are much more attracted to this type of decor than to the sterile, always-identical bedrooms and dining rooms, decorated in "twentieth-century garish," that are offered by most motel chains.

What I'm saying, in other words, is that there is a real vacuum, an overlooked opportunity, in the motel market, and sooner or later somebody is going to step into the gap and make a great deal of money with such a venture.

So how would you get into this business?

First of all, if you like this idea, you have a ready-made property ploy. So all you need is a piece of property. It could be a huge old house that nobody wants—perhaps because the place is too hard to heat. Or the building you're looking for could be one that was used as a small hotel in the past but was put out of business or is on the verge of going out of business because the present owners don't understand how to compete with modern motels.

Of course, it wouldn't do just to pick any old run-down, big building in any part of the country. There are several important factors that you would have to look for. For example, it would be important to be near a major highway, urban center or tourist attraction.

If I were eager to get into this business, I'd get a list of the top one hundred tourist attractions in the United States. One way to do this would be to write to the state tourist bureaus in each state (or in those states that most interest you as a place to live or own property). You might choose Springfield, Illinois, which has numerous shrines to Abraham Lincoln. Or perhaps you would be more interested in San Antonio, with its many Spanish-American sights and historical monuments like the Alamo.

When you've picked your site and purchased your large home or run-down old hotel or boarding house, then you would proceed to fix it up in a way that would appeal to *you* if you were sick and tired of ordinary motel rooms. Then you would list your establishment with national and international accommodations lists as a bed-and-breakfast inn with considerably lower rates than the average motel in your area.

If you and your family do most of the work running and maintaining a place like this, handling eight to twenty rooms, with perhaps one hired maid and in very busy times a part-time cook or kitchen helper, I would be stunned if you failed to make a substantial profit. For one thing, I think you would attract many Americans who are looking for the kind of atmosphere on the road that you could provide. Also, if you happen to have chosen a spot that is frequented by many foreign tourists, especially those from Europe, you would be in a position to offer them a little piece of their home. That sort of familiarity is precisely what many people on a long trip are looking for.

And if you put one of these bed-and-breakfast operations into effect and begin to turn a nice profit, the sky could be the limit after that. You could open another place, hire a local family to take care of it, perhaps give them a percentage of the ownership, and maintain quality control by requiring that they measure up to certain key standards that you have found to be essential in your first effort. If the second one works, then you could be well on your way to establishing a bed-and-breakfast chain, and, of course, the more profit centers like this you develop, the larger your fortune grows.

The first bed-and-breakfast inn you open up could easily be financed by one family of moderate means, especially if they make their home at the same spot. Since the building you would want to choose should be one that nobody else wants, it will most likely be going for a lower price than the better homes in the area. You may well have to do a considerable amount of redecoration and remodeling to get the building up to the standards you've set for yourself. But the total cost should be well within the average family's finances.

Another approach to bargain-basement real estate is to take some special skill you have, such as the expertise you use to make a living or to pursue some personal avocation that you have, and then combine that talent with a real estate purchase.

For example, if you're a teacher by profession or you've had some informal or occasional opportunities to teach others about skills you have, and you've found you're good at it, then you might try something like this: You could get a group of other teachers together, say four or five or more, and purchase a tract of land with a cheap, "purple-tree-in-the-forest" type of building up in Massachusetts, in the hills of North Carolina or in some other similarly rustic location. The type of building you might look for could be another school that has gone out of business. There have been a number of reports recently about a growing glut of these buildings on the market because once they've been designed and built as schools, there's not much else they can be used for. Another possibility would be an abandoned church that most buyers don't want because it's too hard to heat—and, once again, too hard to renovate for other purposes.

What kind of school would you choose to establish in the building you buy? Of course, that's up to you and the direction you feel led by your particular fields of specialization and personal interests.

But as for me, if I were a teacher, I would probably put together the sort of school that I feel is needed as a result of experiences my own children have had in their education. In my opinion, there is a tremendous need for more schools that focus on the basics of education rather than all the expensive "extras" such as special shops, video centers or professional-level athletics facilities.

I could easily see a bunch of teachers getting together with the idea of establishing a boarding school to focus *only* on academic excellence in traditional subjects. As the quality of public education declines in this country— and it seems to me that the decline has been steady in the recent past and will continue to be steady in the foreseeable future—the demand for quality schools of every type will grow.

Quality schools that charge thousands of dollars a year will be seen as the only hope for a decent education for kids in the eyes of many parents. So if you choose your teacher-partners right, do your homework on accreditation and other important procedures, and cut out all the nonessentials in setting up your physical facilities and various programs, you could find yourself sitting on a gold mine almost immediately.

Now some people, including a number of teachers, may object, "But how can you make any money out of education these days?" Or, "That's an old-hat idea. How can an old idea like that possibly make a person any big money?"

I know that this idea is "old" in that it's been done by a number of groups, such as the Montessori schools and others. They have taken one educational concept and spread them around in other sections of the country. But that's exactly what I'm getting at. Remember the bed-and-breakfast example, and think in bigger terms than just one institution. If you start your school and it's successful, then you could start another and another. You in effect would be doing what I call "branchising" your basic program. That's different from a franchise because of requirements for stricter licensing and stricter control over the quality of the product you're offering—in this case, education.

By now we've already gotten to the point of an entire system of schools, and you're probably wondering, "How on earth am I going to finance this?"

But remember: We started off small, and in this case we had several partners investing together. They found a piece of farmland or other tract that probably had been on the market for a while and therefore would have been relatively low in cost. And the building that they discovered, perhaps a huge, rambling farmhouse with a barn, was in many ways a white elephant as well.

Then, with four or more individuals of average means investing together, they could easily have put together $30,000 to $50,000 as seed money. This would go a long way toward convincing a bank that they meant business and should be given a loan to cover the rest of the purchase price and renovations. Their argument would be even stronger since they would be buying the property with the idea of turning it into a business—teaching—that they know a great deal about because it's their life's work.

Now, I know there are problems with a concept like this. For example, are the teachers supposed to give up their tenure at their present jobs and launch an untried idea with their life savings?

I agree that there is some risk here, and it would undoubtedly be necessary for any teachers who are contemplating such a venture as this to do a completely thorough planning job ahead of time and also probably line up students well in advance so that they could be reasonably sure that they had a going proposition before they quit their jobs. There might also be some way to set the school up and then hire superior teachers who for some reason are out of work. Perhaps they have been laid off because of fiscal cutbacks in their area, or they got out of the teaching field voluntarily and are looking for ways to get back into it.

But no matter what property ploy you come up with, there are always problems that arise and objections that can be raised. If you *want* it to happen, however, then you can *make* it happen.

Another low-cost, low-risk type of real estate investment is a variation on what is known these days as "time-sharing." But in using this term I am not suggesting that you get into the type of time-sharing that is offered by many huge real estate firms or developers. There are a number of entrepreneurs around this country, particularly in resort areas like Florida, who are in the process of trying to make a mint by taking old motels along the beaches and in effect selling the rooms to a multitude of individual buyers.

If you go into one of these deals, you typically get one or two weeks each year at an exorbitantly high price, and then other buyers would "buy" the same room for various other weeks during the year. In addition, these deals offer you exchange or substitution rights with resort motels elsewhere in the United States, the Caribbean or other foreign locations.

But there's a better way to go about this and end up with a much more substantial property interest.

I would suggest that you pick an area where you vacation regularly or believe you would prefer to vacation and then find six to twelve other individuals or families who like the same vacation site. Then decide how much you want to spend and start looking for an appropriate piece of property.

If you have twelve people and each is willing to kick in $10,000, you would be in a position to build a very nice property for $120,000. This amount would include a down payment on your land and buildings and also enough left over to do a good job of remodeling the living units to meet your needs. If each person or family is able to invest more—say $20,000—you could get an absolutely *magnificent* piece of property for your combined $240,000. And I'm talking about great property either in a major beach resort area like Florida or a winter sports resort area like the best sections of Vermont.

Of course there are many variations on this approach. If your investors prefer to get involved in a smaller-scale deal, they might invest $5,000 or less and still have enough for a down payment and some renovations on some decent land and a building.

The way this kind of time-sharing would operate would be for each investor to be entitled to a certain amount of time on the property in proportion to the amount of his investment. So if you had twelve investors and each had put in an equal amount of money, each might be entitled to one month on the property. If you had six investors who had contributed equal amounts of money, they would be entitled to two months each, and so forth.

If each investor is only entitled to one or two months, however, it would be necessary to work out some equitable arrangement so that the people who ended up with the least desirable months in any given year would be compensated in some way. For example, the people who got the choice spring or early summer months in Florida might have to pay a larger proportion of the real estate taxes, mortgage payments or some other outlay of costs in that particular year. Then, the next year, the times might be rotated so that each investor would eventually be able to take advantage of one of the better months.

On the other hand, this problem of allocating the months could be obviated completely by building several living units on the land. If you just have one house, then each investor would have to alternate the use of the house. But if you had what amounted to a condominium complex, with six living units for all twelve of your investors, then there would be considerably more flexibility in giving each investor the access to the property during the best vacation months each year.

Before you get involved in any joint investment of this type, there are several important principles to keep in mind. First of all, you should be aware of the advantages of the so-called "brother-in-law rate." This concept refers to the idea that, if possible, you should include in your group of investors people who have special skills that you will need in purchasing or remodeling the property. Then they should be able to contribute their skills at a premium rate or no rate at all in return for their investment interest.

For example, if your personal accountant is a good friend, he might handle all of the accounting aspects of the deal. If you know a real estate lawyer who would be interested in going in with you, you may be able to cut way down on your legal costs. Similarly, friends who are experts in architecture, interior design, or carpentry would be able to reduce your costs still further.

Another important principle is that you should *avoid diversity of interests* among your investors. This means that all of your investors should have the same basic set of goals in buying the property. If your main interest is in developing a personal vacation spot, then all of the investors should have that as their primary goal. One shouldn't want a vacation spot, another an income investment, another a quick profit that might involve selling out after a couple of years, and so on.

A third important principle is that when you get several people going in together on an investment, it's a good idea in preparing to deal with banks, brokers and other professionals and institutions that may be involved in a real estate purchase to *set yourself up as a formal business.* This would involve, at the least, designing some stationery with a nice letterhead giving your group a special name—such as "Suncoast Investors, Inc.," if you happen to be concentrating on Florida real estate.

It's also a good idea to incorporate as a "Subchapter S" corporation. This will only cost you a few hundred dollars, and you will be able to limit your liabilities and divide your interests in the company more easily by issuing shares of stock. In addition, this type of small corporation, which can have a maximum of twenty-five investors and one class of stock, will allow you to "pass through" gains and losses from the business without having to pay a separate corporate income tax.

Having a formal organization, such as a corporation, will also give you more of an official appearance if you have to go outside your circle of immediate friends and acquaintances to get enough investors to make up your total complement of participants in the venture. You'd be amazed at how much more powerful an impact a couple of simple things like a letterhead and a corporate seal can make on supposedly sophisticated people like bankers, brokers and experienced real estate investors!

I could continue *ad infinitum* with examples like these, but I think you get the point. These three ideas—the bed-and-breakfast system, setting up schools on depressed or overlooked property, and time-sharing arrangements in attractive resort areas—are being tried successfully in this country and abroad. You could go out right now and put any of these things into effect if you have the interest, skills and motivation to do it. Or there are dozens, even hundreds of thousands of similar ideas that you could latch onto and "make happen" with equal success and an equally limited amount of capital investment.

The key to success in any real estate venture is not the money—it's the *idea.* If you have the right idea and the character or grim determination to start the wheels rolling and keep them rolling, the money will always be available, either from banks or other excited investors.

* * *

Now, let's move on to another type of rags-to-riches real estate investment that you can take advantage of with either a little or a lot of money—the so-called depressed property that is just waiting to be exploited for profit in many sections of the country.

6

The Depressed
Property Principle

DEPRESSED PROPERTY is property that has lost a part
of its original value because it has become run-down or
unprofitable—perhaps because of poor management, a
changing neighborhood or simply the advanced age of the
structures on the real estate. Unlike the "purple tree in
the forest," which may be totally worthless, depressed
real estate often has some value. But it's definitely on the
decline as a base for a money-making business or as a
sound real estate investment.

Some people take one look at this type of deteriorating
and frequently dilapidated property and immediately reject it as a potential investment vehicle. But the "depressed property principle," which has guided me for
more than a decade now, has convinced me there *is* hope
for many of these tracts of depressed real estate. It's just
a matter of (1) taking that "second look" at depressed
property, (2) trying to see it in a new and more profitable
light, and then (3) putting the land together with an appropriate money-making idea.

One of the most obvious ways of applying this principle is to buy a house that is in bad condition—but in a

relatively good neighborhood. Then you could use your handyman's skills to put it into good shape so that you can sell it for a handsome profit.

The trick here, though, is to pick the right house in the right neighborhood. If you buy a depressed house in a neighborhood that is depressed, especially one where middle-income people are moving out rather than in, you could find yourself with a high-class, beautifully decorated place that nobody wants to buy.

On the other hand, if you find a home that is selling low because it's practically falling apart but that appears to have tremendous potential if it could be upgraded to meet the standards of the surrounding homes, you could be looking at a real rags-to-riches winner. I can think of a couple of examples of how this depressed property principle may work in practice with private homes. Let me mention them briefly, and then we'll move on to much bigger game than the individual house.

One case I know about involved a New York City townhouse that was allowed to deteriorate in the Murray Hill section of Manhattan's East Side. The building, which was a four-story row-house structure on a pleasant street lined with trees, was located in one of Manhattan's nicest areas. The section is not as expensive and exclusive as the upper East Side, where brownstones and townhouses sell for $2 million or more. But a well-maintained home in this part of Murray Hill may go for $700,000 or more, with much lower property taxes than some of the more expensive locations in New York City.

The people who lived in this home bought it for about $90,000 in the mid–1970s. But they lacked the money to do the needed repairs and maintenance on it over the years, and the property steadily deteriorated. At one point, the husband actually stepped through one of the rotted floors on the second-floor stair landing. So the decision was made to sell the building, and a buyer finally came along and purchased it for approximately $500,000 in 1981.

Now, as you can probably see, a couple of important things have been happening with this property. The former owners, even though they were unable to keep the property up, made an extremely wise purchase in that they acquired property at the right time in a neighborhood where land values were in the process of skyrocketing.

But the present owners also got a bargain, even at five times the mid–1970s price, because they knew that with some reasonable efforts at restoration, they would be in a good position to increase the value of the property by several hundred thousand dollars almost immediately. And if they maintained the property in that particular neighborhood, which still shows every sign of becoming one of the best residential areas in Manhattan, their townhouse could be worth millions by the mid–1980s.

But there are also some significant dangers and drawbacks in buying a depressed home with the idea of improving it and selling it at a profit.

First of all, you may guess wrong about the neighborhood: It may *seem* to be on the upswing, but then it may unexpectedly take a plunge and become depressed right along with the home you've bought. For example, I know some people who bought a couple of homes in commuting areas of Long Island because they felt certain that residents of New York City, who were having kids or running into excessively high rents, would want to escape to the suburbs. But then mortgage interest rates went through the roof, and all a sudden people weren't interested in buying homes on Long Island. So these people were stuck with some beautifully remodeled homes that they had spent months working on.

The second problem with upgrading a depressed home is that you have to be very careful how much you spend on your remodeling. It's very easy to spend thousands of dollars bringing a dilapidated house up to par. You may even find when you're finished that you're able to sell the property for much more than you paid for it—but your entire profit may be totally eaten up in remodeling costs! I would estimate, for example, that the Murray Hill townhouse we just discussed would require $100,000 to $200,000 to remodel properly, given New York City's astronomical building costs. If the present owners can resell the building for $800,000 or more in a couple of years, they'll make a nice profit. But if the city's housing market stabilizes or declines, they may be stuck with a high-priced white elephant.

Of course, if you're handy with tools, you may be able to do most of the work yourself and save the expense of bringing in professional carpenters and other experts. But remember: If you do the work yourself, you're going to be putting in a great deal of time that you could be spending on other real estate enterprises. It's important to ask yourself periodically in your real estate ventures, "How much is my time really worth?" Otherwise, you may find that you're wasting your energies on relatively unproductive projects.

And that brings me to my third point: I think upgrading a home may be a nice hobby, but I really don't recommend it as a way to make a fortune in depressed real estate in the present economy. Instead, I would advise you to turn your creativity in other directions—especially toward depressed *business* properties.

There are many possibilities for finding a run-down or declining business and using your special skills and ideas to turn it around and make a lot of money out of it. Let me show you what I'm talking about through a case study involving one of my own depressed real estate ventures.

In the course of my expanding real estate dealings, I noticed that some big motel chains, especially Holiday Inn of America, regularly were putting up their "mature" or older properties for sale. In the case of Holiday Inn, if they kept these old motels in their system, it would have taken a great deal of money to remodel them. You see, they have a set of corporate criteria in terms of the style of a room, and some of the older properties, which had been around for ten or fifteen years, were too "mature" to meet contemporary standards.

At the time, I knew nothing about the motel or hotel business. But I did know how to ask good questions. So I began to seek out friends of mine who did have some expertise. I asked them, "What do you think of those old Holiday Inn rooms? If the room rates were discounted, could they compete in today's market? How much do you think it would take to get them in decent shape? What about the underlying electric and plumbing systems—are they sound? Would you consider buying any of them if you had the money?"

Before long, this preliminary research taught me a great deal about the motel business, and I became convinced that it was possible to make a lot of money on some of those "depressed" properties, provided the owner took just the right approach. The approach I finally decided on was to turn them into a completely different concept: the "luxury budget" motel. The rooms would be more expensive than the cheapest budget units, like those offered by a chain like Day's Inns. But at the same time, they would be more economical than a Holiday Inn or a Ramada Inn.

After a little more personal research, I learned that I could remodel many of the old Holiday Inn properties for about $50,000 and bring them up to my luxury budget standard that I was thinking about. In contrast, it would have cost about $500,000 to raise them to the level that Holiday Inn required for its properties.

So all the spadework had been done. What I needed was the right kind of motel that I could use to try out my depressed property principle. Then, I heard through one of my business contacts that Holiday Inn was planning to sell off several hundred of their older properties, and I immediately went on the offensive. I went directly to the main corporate offices in Memphis, Tennessee, and said, "Look, I'd like to buy some of those problem motels. You're trying to get rid of them, and I'd like to be your garbage can."

Now, at the time I had considerable personal holdings in other real estate investments, including some billboard companies. But even though I knew I had access to personal funds and also good contacts with potential investors, the Holiday Inn people didn't know me from Adam.

And this is an important point for you to keep in mind. If you hear about a good deal in depressed property that you think you could turn into a nice profit, don't be shy about trying to acquire it! Above all, don't let the fact that a big corporation may be the owner scare you away. They are often motivated to sell mature or surplus assets because of *aesthetic* reasons, not because the facility is losing money. On the contrary, very often a corporately owned motel or restaurant which is turning a profit may still be put up for sale because its facilities or facade are out-of-date. But an enterprising individual can then rehabilitate it, return it to the system and find himself holding a much more valuable property than he originally bought.

For example, I've never been in touch with the corporate headquarters of McDonald's or Burger King. But I'll bet you that right now some of their older properties are in trouble. Let's say they've got a number of locations that we'd classify as "depressed," and you have an idea—a promising property ploy—for using their real estate for some new purpose. You could easily pick up the phone, call their headquarters, and tell them the crux of your idea and how you can get the financing to pull it off. I'll bet there's a better than even chance they'd say, "Come on down! Let's talk some more about this!"

An associate of mine did this very thing with the Stuckey restaurant chain, which is owned by Pet Milk and has highway outlets all over the South. He had noticed that some of their restaurants only had two or three cars in front of them during the height of the tourist season, and that meant something was wrong with those particular locations.

So he got on the phone to the Pet Milk Company's corporate headquarters and talked to an officer who was in charge of the Stuckey's division. He's now in the midst of negotiating for some of those lagging outlets and hoping to turn them into a more profitable kind of highway restaurant.

One important lesson here is that if you make a call to a big company like this, you want to talk to the highest-ranking officer who is involved in the actual operations of the stores or restaurants you're interested in. It doesn't help much to shoot too high—say, for the chairman of the board of Pet Milk—because you'll probably never get through to him. And if you do, he'll just refer you back to the top operating officer.

On the other hand if you shoot too low—if you go to talk to someone at the regional management level—your efforts will most likely be just as fruitless. In these lower offices, you're likely to be referred to a youngster who will pretend to have authority but who really doesn't and may string you along and waste your time before you realize what is happening.

Or you may run into the older guy, with crew cut and white socks, who cuts you off with something like, "We don't have no problems!" This type of person would be too defensive and too caught up in superficial company loyalty to be any help. He's probably got the corporate seal tattooed on his bottom, and there's no way he's going to let someone he perceives as an unorthodox entre-preneur get past him.

These were some of the considerations I had in mind when I approached some officers in the corporate head-quarters of Holiday Inn. And as it turned out, I contacted the right people because they immediately offered me three "mature"—or what I would call depressed—Holi-day Inns: one in Houston, Texas; one in Hattiesburg, Mis-sissippi; and one in Oak Ridge, Tennessee. Now, the motel I *really* wanted among those three was the one in Oak Ridge because I felt that, despite its old and run-down condition, it was in an excellent location if the motel plant could be sufficiently upgraded. Oak Ridge, you see, is often referred to as the "energy capital of the world" because much of the research in nuclear power has gone on there since the building of the first atom bomb. Top-level scientists, corporate executives, and foreign digni-taries come in and out of the town regularly, and they needed a better place to stay than what the other hotels and motels could offer.

The other two properties were located in sections of Houston and Hattiesburg that I felt were not upwardly mobile, and so I wasn't as interested in them. But if I had to take them on to get the one at Oak Ridge, I was ready to consider it.

The first big problem we ran into, however, was the method of financing. I thought I'd try to buy the proper-ties through another corporation in which I owned about 25 percent of the stock. But this company was having some financial problems itself, and if we went that route, Holiday Inn insisted that I personally guarantee an obligation of $2.6 million, which was the asking price for the three motels.

As I mentioned earlier, I don't mind personally guaranteeing a note if I'm the borrower. But in this case, I would have been only a cosigner. I wouldn't have had a right to any of the equity or potential capital growth in the motels, except indirectly, to the extent that I owned 25 percent of the stock of the other company.

So we went back to the drawing boards on the financing. Finally, we reached an agreement whereby I put up $100,000 for the three properties. I also gave Holiday Inn a series of "cross guarantees" by which I would assume an outstanding bank note on the Houston property amounting to $1,145,000.

So I bought the Houston motel for $1,250,000; the Hattiesburg property for $550,000; and the motel in Oak Ridge for $775,000. The total, which I was able to acquire for that $100,000 initial investment, came to just a little less than $2.6 million.

The Hattiesburg motel was financed by a savings and loan association in Jackson, Mississippi, with a $400,000 first mortgage. Holiday Inn took back a second mortgage of $150,000 to be repaid over five years. The Oak Ridge motel was financed by a $575,000 first mortgage from the Bank of Oak Ridge. Holiday Inn took back a second mortgage of $200,000 for five years.

I used the income produced by the Houston and Hattiesburg properties to maintain them until I could find a suitable buyer. At the same time, I concentrated my major remodeling efforts on the Oak Ridge motel, because I saw it as the depressed real estate with the greatest potential. During the six years I owned the Oak Ridge location, I put about $350,000 into these efforts to upgrade its facilities.

As I said, all three of those properties were depressed in the sense that by some tests they seemed over-the-hill as profitable motels. The Hattiesburg, Mississippi, location had already been bypassed by an interstate highway, and I didn't feel I had sufficient knowledge of the area to make it as profitable as I liked. So I just sat on it for about two years and kept it in reasonably good condition, with a few strategic paint jobs and room repairs to raise it slightly above the level at which I had bought it. In this way, I was able to sell it only two years later to someone who *did* know the area—at a profit of about $200,000.

As for the Houston motel, it was evident to me that this location was in an area of a city that was on the decline, even though it was situated right on an interstate highway. Also, even though the place had good visibility from the highway, it was hard for motorists to get to because of the configuration of highway exits. In addition to these problems, the motel had enormously high payroll costs, and the low rate of unemployment in Houston, which was a result of the great availability of jobs in a booming local economy, meant it was hard to hold good people unless you paid them exceptionally well.

So I was at least as eager to get out of the Houston property as the one in Hattiesburg. In this case, the opportunity came along in only about a year and a half. An interested buyer appeared, and I made a profit of approximately $150,000 on the sale.

As was the situation with the Mississippi motel, I just maintained the Houston building at a certain level and improved it a little bit, here and there, without doing any major remodeling. And that represents an important principle to remember about any property you hope to resell: You always have to put in a certain amount of money just to keep your building and grounds at the level at which you bought them. Otherwise, you'll make the depressed property you've purchased even *more* depressed, and you may well end up selling it at a loss.

The best approach is to put in a *little* more than the bare minimum required for basic maintenance so that you enhance the appearance and usability of the property, even if ever so slightly. If you do this, there's a good chance you can sell later at a nice profit, provided the surrounding neighborhood doesn't go into a nosedive.

But the really big money in depressed real estate requires more of a effort at renovation than I tried with either the Houston or Hattiesburg motel. After completing the sales of those two properties, I concentrated all my efforts on upgrading the Oak Ridge facility, which I saw as my piece of depressed real estate with the greatest profit potential.

I applied to Holiday Inn of America for a franchise and after a great deal of market analysis and feasibility studies, they offered me a franchise if I would upgrade the property to the new Holiday Inn standards. I immediately decided to take advantage of this opportunity because I knew that having the strongest franchise label in the industry would certainly increase the future value of the property.

As I said before, I pumped about $350,000 into that motel to give it the nicest accommodations for travelers I could achieve, and I found the Holiday Inn company to be most helpful, encouraging and equitable during the transition period. Then, I began to watch for potential buyers, and they weren't long in appearing since I had managed to become a successful member of the Holiday Inn system.

The first significant overtures that I had, from people who were really interested in purchasing the property, came after I put the word out that I wasn't really committed to the motel business and that I was looking for a buyer. Several people and groups approached me, but the most persistent was a fellow named Phil Miller, who is the most successful broker of Holiday Inn in the United States.

Miller, who found out about my property through a mutual friend, phoned me to see if we could get together to talk about a possible deal. The thing that impressed me first about Miller was that he had done his homework. As a matter of fact, when I did meet him face to face, I learned he had already been to see my property at Oak Ridge. I didn't have to tell him the strengths and weaknesses of the motel—he told me!

For example, I knew the people who were managing my property had some weaknesses in their business abilities. Also, I knew that there was a lack of control of waitresses and other employees in their relationships with customers. Part of the problem was that I was living in Atlanta and working on other enterprises there, and the motel was located a several hours' drive north in Tennessee.

But Miller already knew about these problems and others, so I didn't have to give him much of an introduction to the real estate. Instead, we got down to hard negotiating almost immediately. I told him right off, "The motel's for sale for $3.2 million. I want $700,000 down, and then $2.5 million amortized over twenty years, with a balloon at the end of ten years." A "balloon," by the way, is a large final payment that allows a buyer to make relatively low payments over ten years and then pay the final amount in a larger lump sum at the end of that period.

As I expected, he didn't go for that immediately—especially not the size of the down payment. He had a potential buyer in mind, and it turned out he would be representing the buyer, who would pay his brokerage fee.

But until he and I could arrive at a tentative understanding, there would be no use in bringing the buyer into the discussions.

Miller and I continued our talks for several months, and the best way I can describe his approach is that he alternately wooed and bullied me. He moved so fast in so many different directions that one day I'd be suspicious of him or even hate him, and the next I'd think he might become one of my best friends.

On one occasion he took it upon himself to do what amounted to a full-scale study of the motel and our relationships with corporations and local government officials in the Oak Ridge community. For example, he went to the Union Carbide Company, our largest clients, and asked them what their reaction was to our place. He found out what was good about our operation but also what was bad. And then he'd hit me directly with a criticism a client might have of our service.

He kept trying to drive my enthusiasm for the property down, down, down in an effort to get me to say, in effect, "I give up! I'll sell, I'll sell!" More often than not, those criticisms of his would focus on problems I couldn't do anything about because I was working in Atlanta 200 miles away.

Another time he talked to an important official in one of the major civic groups, and then he began to tell me about what a "jewel" this woman was. What he was doing was letting me know that he had a real personal relationship with a person who held a key position in that community. As a matter of fact, I had never met her, and he was aware of that. And that was another good piece of salesmanship. I owned the property, and he was an outside broker—yet he already had contacts in the community that I didn't have.

He was a great salesman, but I know something about

good salesmanship too. So even though he was beginning to weaken my defenses, I didn't let him know it. I just tried to drive him a little crazy by responding, "Phil, I really don't care about that." Or, "What's any of that got to do with me?"

I think he fully expected me to become shocked or disturbed or to collapse in tears at the revelations he was giving me. But I'd just keep a dead-pan expression and perhaps respond, "That's really a petty problem as far as I'm concerned. But if your clients buy this property, it'll be their big opportunity."

But perhaps the most dramatic ploy he used was when he made a special trip down to Atlanta to run for a week with my personal running coach. This coach, Mike Spino, was originally from New Jersey, had a background in Zen techniques and was an expert in mind and body fitness. I had developed some leg cramps and coldness in one leg, and the coach was trying to help me with that problem as well as keep me in generally good shape.

Well, before long, Miller was telling me about his leg cramps and the coldness in his leg. He also mentioned that he had been working with my coach, and then he started sending all sorts of mind-relaxing tapes on how to get rid of stress.

During one of my next sessions with the running coach, I said, "You've been seeing Phil Miller?"

"Bill, I don't want to get in the middle of that one," he said. "I really don't want to get between you two guys."

And I let the matter drop with that. But I was amused and even more impressed by Miller's tenacity. I decided right then that if I ever had an important property I wanted to sell and I felt I needed a broker, Phil Miller would be the guy I'd seek out first to handle the deal.

And I'd say that's something for you to keep in mind too. If you start dealing seriously in real estate, you'll eventually have to work with a broker. But when you go about evaluating his ability, look for some of the qualities I found in Miller: thoroughness, a broad knowledge of the pros and cons of owning certain types of property, and the persistence to stick with a potential deal until he "makes it happen."

On this last point, I'm fully convinced that there wouldn't have been a sale of my motel at that time if Miller hadn't been involved. He was really the key person who finally "made it happen" because the deal almost fell apart after I got together with the prospective buyers.

Miller had gotten me *down* to the bare minimum I was willing to accept, and I expect that he had gotten the buyers, a couple of brothers from the Midwest named Cahill, *up* to the highest price they were willing to pay. The problem was that, unknown to either of us parties, we weren't exactly in agreement when Miller decided to put us together to hammer out the final deal.

I liked the spokesman for the buyers, Larry Cahill, right away, and I could tell immediately that he knew his business. His company had bought about twenty Holiday Inns in the past, and he seemed certain that he could take my property and do more with it than I had. But he wasn't cocky—at least, not in the way I'm sometimes accused of being. He had a lot of humility about his achievements and also an openness that enabled him always to look you straight in the eye and tell you exactly what he wanted and what he was willing to do to get it.

Larry Cahill was obviously a man to be trusted and not a man whom you played games with when you were ready to sew up a deal. That was part of the problem that developed when we all assembled in the law offices of a big Atlanta firm. You see, not all the details had been nailed down, partly because the broker was trying to iron out a few final points and partly because the deal was potentially so complex that the attorneys were trying to cross every "t" and dot every "i."

I think Phil Miller knew that there were still some important points that the two sides weren't in complete accord on, and he felt if we could meet face to face we would have a better chance of consummating the contract than if we negotiated through him long distance. So he came into Atlanta on the morning of the meeting, but without anything committed to writing, and in a whirlwind of activity put the arm on my secretary and started drafting up a purchase agreement.

Miller was more or less acting as the mediator and facilitator between two attorneys: my personal lawyer and good friend, Dick Hammel, a C.P.A. and attorney who practices in Milwaukee; and the personal attorney for the Cahills, Al Ross, from Arlington, Texas. But all three of those guys were used to putting together big deals in a minimum amount of time, and so it didn't take long for them to come up with a draft.

The big problem surfaced when I decided for several reasons that we should go to a larger law firm I had used for much of my other legal work. We had a lot of other people coming in from the Cahill company later that day for the final signing, and I figured we should have a bigger conference table, which the law firm could offer. Also, the deal had become so complex that at the time, I thought I would be more comfortable with all the backup attorneys, library facilities, word-processing equipment and other aids that the big firm could offer.

But that turned out to be a mistake—a mistake that almost destroyed the entire deal. And I think there are a number of lessons that any real estate investor can learn from my experience.

First of all, it's important to choose the right lawyer for the right deal. You'll be working with attorneys as you get involved in more lucrative rags-to-riches real estate transactions. But always ask yourself, "Will this lawyer or this law firm fit in with the parties in this deal and what we're trying to accomplish?"

The difficulty in making this determination is that sometimes you may have reason to be suspicious of a person or company you're dealing with. Or perhaps there is a tendency on the part of the other party to try to cover even the most minor points and contingencies in a contract.

Now, normally, I wouldn't want to deal at all with a person or company I didn't trust. But sometimes, if you want to sell a property, you *have* to negotiate with people you don't particularly like or respect. In those cases, it's important to bring out all the heavy artillery that a big law firm or leading legal specialist can offer.

But in this Holiday Inn case, we had a different situation. There, we were going to commit the important points to writing. But at the same time, there was a "handshake" atmosphere about the deal as it was developing. I knew there were many points, about payment of the purchase price and my getting certain percentages of their sales, that required me to trust them up to a point. Otherwise, I would be forced to have my attorneys draft a fifty-page document that would take weeks or months to work out.

But it soon became apparent, when we arrived at the big law offices, that this meticulous approach wasn't called for here. I've already said that Larry Cahill, the main man on the other side, was a straightforward, straight-shooting businessman. He walked into those law offices, listened to some of the preliminary legal skirmishing and nit-picking and said, "I came here today thinking we were going to sign something."

It was that simple. He didn't say, "Well, it was my

anticipation that certain relevant documents would be prepared for my consideration, and then we would be able to proceed with further negotiations . . ."

No, none of that gobbledygook for Cahill. He just said, "I came here to sign."

During the next couple of hours, my associates and I did a lot of talking and then were absent from the conference room for long periods. But I could sense when we returned that our prospective buyers were getting more and more frustrated. I was sensitive to their feelings because I had been in their shoes as a buyer in other deals in the past.

So it became obvious to me and my advisers, particularly Dick Hammel, that if we hoped to reach an agreement, it had to be done in a less formal setting, with fewer legal barriers to our business negotiations. And that reminds me of another important point to keep in mind about an attorney: You should choose one who understands the difference between the *legal* and the *business* aspects of a deal. Too often, lawyers get too involved and their legal work tends to spill over too much into what should be primarily the business considerations of a property negotiation.

So remember: Even though you should listen closely to your attorney because he certainly knows the law better than you do, in the last analysis it's up to you, as the *employer* of the lawyer, to exercise ultimate control. Every deal has a certain pace and momentum to it. Some take longer to complete than others. But if you allow things to slow down too much, you may well find yourself coming up empty-handed and disappointed.

Phil Miller, the broker, understood this principle quite well, and he finally stepped in and began to stage-manage the entire meeting. I've seen a lot of hotshot negotiators in my time, but I've never seen one who could match

Miller's performance in those final moments. He saw the deal falling apart, and so he edged his way into a seat at the head of this long conference table—a position that gave him the most powerful, commanding physical position in the room—and he began to perform.

I had been feeling a lot of pressure that afternoon because it had been my idea to use the big law firm, and I was having to make all of the final decisions about contract proposals that were coming from the other side. Miller apparently sensed the pressure on me and decided to apply a little more. He said, "How about you, Bill, do you want to close this deal today?"

Now, that's putting it right to you. There I was, in the middle of more than a dozen frustrated, high-powered businessmen, and the ball was squarely in my court. If I had answered, "Yes!" too quickly, that would have been bad because it would have given the impression that I was too eager. They could have gotten the idea that I was sick and tired of the whole thing and would sell on any basis. Or they might have thought I was in effect saying, "Yes, I want your money, and I want to go to the bank this afternoon with it because I'm really selling you a bomb!"

Or course, neither of those conclusions would have been true. I *was* tired and ready to close the deal. But at the same time I was quite ready to walk out if we couldn't come to terms. And I certainly didn't think I was selling them any bomb. I knew what the property was worth, and I thought that the general terms we were talking about would be fair to both sides.

So I hedged a little in answering Miller's question. I said, "Yes, I want to close, but the main reason is that I have several other properties I'm trying to sell in the next few weeks. If this one drags on, these negotiations could get in the way of the others."

So I tossed the ball right back at Miller, but he wasn't

about to let me get off that easily. He asked, pressing once more, "So you want to close today then, Bill?"

"Sure, if we can," I replied. "But what about you, Larry?" I asked, throwing the ball into the lap of the main Cahill spokesman.

"I came here today to close," he said. "I expected to see final documents. I want to sign and get going."

Well, that was the answer. And once again, Miller took the lead. He said, "Okay, boys, let's get out of here and find a place where we can talk and close this deal."

So we all went back to my office, found a photocopy machine and a typewriter and put the final contract together by midnight that same night. Although the final document was only a few pages long, it represented a rather complex arrangement. Let me explain a few of the broad outlines of the deal:

I decided to lease them the property for forty-nine years rather than sell it—for a number of reasons, which I'll discuss in a later chapter that deals specifically with the advantages of leasing. They bought the motel buildings situated on about four acres of land in Oak Ridge, and I withheld a vacant acre-and-a-half because I figured it might be used for apartments or commercial use in a few years.

The price the Cahills paid me for the buildings and contents was $2,750,000. I received a check for $500,000 as a down payment at the time we signed the contract and also a note for $2,250,000 which is to be amortized over twenty years, at 12.5 percent interest.

Also, at the end of that ten-year period, I am to receive an additional payment of principal of about $1.3 million in one lump sum. That's an example of what I've called a balloon payment, which is sometimes tacked on at the end after a buyer has had a number of years to make his property profitable.

The contract also provided for me to receive a minimum of $50,000 a year for the forty-nine years of the lease as a form of rent. This figure would then be changed to $50,000 or 4 percent of room sales, whichever was larger, after ten years. I figured that the Cahills' management company would be able to get those room sales up to at least $2 million annually in ten years, and so my rent based on 4 percent of those sales could easily rise to above $50,000 per year.

As you can see, this was a very profitable transaction, and I am happy to report that the buyers remain extremely happy with their purchase.

But this is by no means the end of this rather lengthy story. I still had a few financial loose ends to tie up, and they involved almost as much real estate cliff-hanging as the primary negotiations. You see, I had a $950,000 note that was outstanding with the Bank of Oak Ridge on the motel, and their approval of the buyer had to be obtained. Although Oak Ridge is a small town, I have always found the officers of this bank to be most professional and far more business-minded than big-city lenders.

Now, I could have paid off that note if I had been forced to by rearranging some of my other bank accounts and capital assets. But no matter who you are, it's best not to have to pay off nearly a million dollars all at once if you can help it. And it's not necessary if a good relationship with the bank exists.

As it happened, the Bank of Oak Ridge officials were gratified to know that buyers with professional Holiday Inn experience had bought the motel. So I arranged for my buyers, the Cahills, to drop by the bank with their top people just to assure the bankers that they were reputable people who were going to make their payments to me on time. I, in turn, could then have the means to make my payments to the bank. The Cahills were apparently impressed by the friendliness at the bank, and they immediately opened several operating accounts themselves.

But that sort of introduction could only go so far. The second thing I had to do was to demonstrate to the bankers in some concrete fashion that I planned to leave part of my liquid assets within easy reach of them. In that way they would readily have a means of recovering their money if I started to run into problems meeting the payments on my note.

The first thing I did was to inform the bankers that I was planning on keeping a bank account with them that I would use to funnel the $31,500 a month I would be receiving from the buyers. I would also arrange to have an automatic monthly debit of that money in the amount of about $14,000 to pay off my mortgage since my loan had fourteen years remaining before it would be paid off. That would provide some automatic security for the bank.

As a matter of fact, even though I no longer have an operating business in Oak Ridge, I plan to continue to purchase certificates of deposit with this bank, and I also expect to purchase shares of its stock. The bank is well-managed and has enormous potential for profit and growth.

This brings the Holiday Inn saga to a close. But as you can see, there are many lessons to be learned about the depressed property principle from a deal like this.

In the first place, it was up to me to find and take a risk on that particular depressed real estate that comprised the Oak Ridge motel. I doubt that the broker Phil Miller or the Cahill company would have bothered with the property as it originally stood because they didn't specialize in motels that looked that bad. But depressed real estate with rags-to-riches potential is something that's quite dear to my Irish heart. So, despite the inadequate knowledge I had of the motel business when I started out,

I was at least in a position to see the possibilities in that depressed property. I was also ready to devote my money and energy to upgrade it so that somebody like Cahill or Miller *would* take a look.

In this little scenario, we've also examined some principles of dealing with brokers and lawyers in a real estate transaction. And perhaps most important of all, we've observed a few actual real estate negotiations and seen the dynamics of how the buyers, sellers and brokers may interact with one another.

Now let me conclude this discussion of the depressed property principle by stressing how essential I feel it is to *narrow* your focus when you're out looking for a rags-to-riches opportunity. There are many types of undervalued property opportunities. But there are also countless other real estate ventures that don't involve depressed, neglected or overlooked property opportunities.

To put it in more personal terms, I could have held onto that motel and tried to do with it what I expect the Cahills will do—turn it into one of the finest facilities in that part of the country. But that's not my main function in the real estate business. It's not my specialty. And *you have to have a specialty,* you have to narrow your focus, if you hope to succeed in business.

If you have a great deal of money, then you can go out looking for properties that have been upgraded to a reasonable level, as the Cahills are doing, and try to make them even more profitable. But for a person of modest means, especially in this uncertain economy, it's much wiser to concentrate on the dregs of the real estate market, on the sow's ears that you can turn into silk purses.

Now, I realize that some aspects of this Holiday Inn transaction involved a lot of money on my part. But if you'll recall, I originally purchased those three Holiday Inns, in Mississippi, Texas and Tennessee, with only

$100,000 down. Of course, I also had to take out a lot of loans and guarantee some notes. But the point I'm making is that the initial capital investment wasn't that great.

You may not be able to come up with $100,000 right now. But I'm quite certain if you learn something about this depressed property business and come up with a good property ploy, you'll be able to find a few associates who are willing to go in with you and find or develop a deal just as I was able to do in Oak Ridge.

And if you decide to put your money on an over-the-hill Holiday Inn, you may just find a hotshot broker like Phil Miller knocking on your door before too long!

Up to this point we've been considering real estate that appears to be useless, hopelessly ugly, or so run-down it has little potential for future profit. There's another category of rags-to-riches property, however, which may be just as neglected but has at least as high a potential for profit. I'm referring to a vast category of *overlooked* uses of property that most people don't think twice about but a few use to make millions.

7

The Great
Billboard Secret

I'VE ALREADY MENTIONED several times that the crown jewel in my own real estate investments is the billboard business. But so far I haven't explained in a practical way how you may be able to make use of an often overlooked concept like this to make some money yourself.

Billboards are in many ways a strange sort of real estate venture. Most people are aware of them as they drive down the nation's highways. They frequently find them to be helpful in locating a good restaurant or motel. Or passengers may play alphabet games with their children by searching through the letters on the advertising that the billboards carry. In some cases, activists may get quite angry and militant because they feel too many signs along the roadways destroy the beauty of the landscape.

But regardless of the varying reactions to billboards, it seems likely that they are here to stay, at least for the foreseeable future. And I find them to be an extremely important and lucrative part of my own ongoing business enterprises. In fact, as I've been working on this very book, I've sold out one billboard company for more than

$5 million, and I'm seriously considering two or three other extremely attractive billboard ventures.

So how do you go about making money in that often overlooked real estate area, billboard advertising? You already know how I got started, as an auditor for the Outdoor Advertising Association of America, which is the national billboard advertising trade association. But that was a method that was special to me and wouldn't work with most other people, especially not those who have a regular job they're holding down in another field.

For the majority of potential billboard investors, I think there are really three ways to go about getting into this type of real estate.

First of all, you could make friends with a going billboard entrepreneur—or a fledgling operator who seems to have great promise—and simply put up some money for his next venture. If he is successful, you could get some significant tax shelters from your investment, as well as a healthy cash flow.

This is the easiest way to get into the billboard industry, but it's also the way in which you exercise the least control over your investment. You just put your money in and hope for the best. Still, I would recommend this approach if you know your billboard operator quite well and he has a good track record of accomplishment in the industry (or, if he's a new entrepreneur, he has done well in some other self-employed real estate field).

The second approach—putting up full-size twelve-by-twenty-four-foot billboards, or poster panels—is the most difficult because it requires the ability to manage several employees and, often, to compete effectively with other experienced operators. It's also the most expensive way to get into the business.

But if you can place a fairly large number of boards in good, high-traffic locations with excellent visibility, this method will probably make your operation most attractive to national advertisers, who are willing to pay the highest prices for space.

The third way of getting into the billboard business is by setting up "junior poster panels," or small-size billboards that measure only six by twelve feet. I would recommend this approach for most investors who have an average amount of capital to invest and who want to limit their management commitment to only one or two employees or partners.

But now let's get more specific. I want to describe to you in some detail exactly what the often overlooked billboard approach to real estate investment involves. Then you can decide for yourself whether you want to become just an investor or a participant with either the regular-size boards or the junior panels.

First of all, I've mentioned this point when we've discussed some of the other forms of rags-to-riches real estate investment, but I'll say it again: If you're going to get into any sort of property investment, do some homework first!

Go visit a few billboard companies (their names should be printed somewhere at the bottom of the billboards in your area); get one of the trade magazines; and check references to the field in your local library. Make a few personal contacts, and try to find out how much money, time and manpower it will take to put up some signs in your locality; also, determine how much income they are likely to generate for you. You can also get some of this information through brochures and other literature available from the Institute of Outdoor Advertising, a national organization for billboard operators.

After you've done some of this preliminary spadework, the time has arrived to put your time and money on the line. It's possible to start a junior panel business out of your garage. But if you're serious about turning this type of real estate investment into a fortune, you'll have to plan on outgrowing your own home as quickly as possible. And you'll also have to think in terms of making this business your main outside activity unless you have a partner who plans to be quite active.

As a matter of fact, someone, either you or your partner or both of you, will eventually have to move into a full-time commitment with the billboard venture if you are to be as successful as I believe you can be. Otherwise, if you try to keep the thing going as a sideline, you'll remain a small-time operator and you'll find that you're putting in too much time (even if it's only part of your time) for too little profit.

Now, I realize these are tough words. But being a successful active investor in your own billboard company will eventually require most or all of your time—at least until you get the business going so well that you can hire a manager to keep it spinning along for you. The most lucrative contracts, the national advertisers, look for a fairly large operation before they'll sit down to talk contracts. The person with one billboard here and one there just doesn't have the leverage to compete for this national advertising. And as a result, his profit potential is severely limited.

So to summarize, I'd say there are two key things to keep in mind if you hope to be successful in the billboard end of the real estate business—or in any other rags-to-riches property venture: The two *worst* things that an entrepreneur can do are (1) to be undercapitalized, so that he runs out of cash before he really gets the business going; and (2) to be unable to make a sufficient commitment of his time, with the result that he doesn't properly oversee the development of his business.

So if you want to succeed in this field, resolve right now that you're going to put in enough time and money to get high visibility in your community and be a real force in the market you've chosen. You have to be a real contender, or you're almost certain to become a mere dilettante.

Now let's take a closer look at what it takes to be a contender in the tougher of the two markets, the regular-size billboard business. Then, we'll go into even more detail with the junior-panel approach to billboard investing.

The Regular-Size Billboard Business

As I mentioned, the large billboards you generally see on roads around the country are the standard twelve by twenty-four feet in size. They each cost about $3,000 per face to put up—and that figure includes all materials and labor. But here's the hitch, as far as the cost is concerned: If you plan to set up your own billboard business and be a real contender in your local market, you will probably need at least 200 of these boards to make a sufficient impact to attract the national advertisers.

So you can see what's happening here: Bang! Right away the entrepreneur has to be in a position to raise $600,000 to make a serious effort in the large billboard market. That might involve $50,000 of his own money; plus another $100,000 raised from friends and acquaintances who want to invest at a certain rate of interest. With this start-up capital of $150,000, he would be in a position to go into a bank and negotiate for the additional $450,000 to get this real estate venture off the ground.

But these are only the very basic capital costs that are involved with large billboards. There is also the question of operating expenses, including renting a space to do the paperwork and providing a staging area to handle the materials needed to put up the billboards. In addition, you always have to figure how much time it's going to take to manage an office and a half-dozen or so employees.

The basic staff you'd need for a large-size billboard operation would include:

A *secretary,* who would perform all the usual secretarial functions. He or she should also be able to assist you in expediting contracts and other legal documents with prospective advertising clients and lessors who would be providing part of their land for you to erect your boards.

A *salesperson,* who actually goes out and contacts advertisers or their agencies to get display contracts for their products.

A *lease person,* who arranges for the leasing of land from the property owners who own the locations where you hope to place your boards. This individual should have a good working knowledge of the building codes in all the communities in your market, and he should also know the building inspectors and how they operate.

Finally, even though almost all of the land a billboard operator uses will be leased, there will be an occasional strip or sliver that may make a good buy for several reasons. For example, perhaps the location is such an ideal, high-traffic area for a billboard that a purchase is warranted. Or perhaps the land strip seems to have future promise as a key to putting other tracts of land in the area together into some sort of development, like a shopping center. In other words, if you hold one strip that a developer must have to consolidate several other lots, you'll be in a strong position to negotiate a sale of your relatively small portion of land at a relatively high price.

Just recently, one of my own lease men proved his value in this regard for my own business. While he was out riding around, looking for possible sites, he learned about a strip of property that was for sale on a well-traveled roadway. By almost anybody's standards, the land was a real white elephant, since it only measured 20 by 150 feet. After all, what could you possibly do with a sliver of land that size? Probably nothing—except erect a highly lucrative billboard on it!

My lease man immediately saw the potential, and he informed me about it. I learned that the land could be bought for only $8,000, and so I got in touch with the owner and closed the deal as quickly as possible. Then, I got in touch with a local advertising company and leased that land to them for $1,800 a year for several of their billboards!

But you certainly don't need a lease man to find this sort of property for you. You can easily do it yourself if you keep your eyes open and take some time to learn what makes a good billboard site and what doesn't. Even the most inexperienced person could see that there was a fair amount of traffic along that highway and that the strip of land in question was easily visible for hundreds of feet to motorists. That's all you really need to know to begin looking seriously at a property for billboard purposes.

So even though your lease person's main specialty should be leases, he or she should also have a feel for a much wider variety of real estate opportunities so that he can keep you in touch with other rags-to-riches possibilities.

The *operations person* is the individual who handles (a) the purchasing of the physical materials you need to put up the billboards; (b) the negotiation and final acceptance of contracts from both advertisers and lessors; and (c) the payment of rents to those landowners who are leasing space to you for your billboards. The actual construction of the billboards can be contracted out to companies that specialize in that sort of thing.

The *billposter* is the individual who actually puts the big advertising sheets up on the billboards.

But the most important actor in this billboard scenario is the entrepreneur himself—in other words, *you*—because if you are in the large-size billboard market, you've got at least $600,000 riding on your venture. That's too much money to be spending unless you're willing to put in a considerable amount of time to stage-manage the show. And if you are involved in your first billboard attempt, it's even more crucial to set aside plenty of time because you'll have to learn some fundamentals that old-time operators already know from past experience.

Ideally, I always recommend that it's best for the entrepreneur to be the company's specialist in advertising and marketing because those are the main fields on which the entire enterprise may stand or fall.

The big billboards themselves are available in kit form from several manufacturers. You might check with some local sign companies to see if they can give you leads about the best companies to contact in your area. These kits consist of a series of steel sections that measure twenty-four feet in length and two feet in width. So, six of these sections, laid immediately above one another horizontally, will measure twelve feet by twenty-four feet —or the size of one large billboard.

Then there's a trim of about ten inches that goes around the basic rectangular structure to give it a picture-frame look. And a few pieces of hardware, including some struts or tie-rods, can be attached to the back to hold the whole thing together. Finally, the entire face of the billboard structure is mounted on two twelve-inch steel beams, about forty feet in length.

When the structure is put up on the land you're leasing, ten feet of those beams is inserted into a concrete foundation in the ground, and thirty feet remains above to support and display the metal facing that will be pasted up with the billboard poster. The most economical way to use this structure, by the way, is to attach *two* billboard facings on the same two steel beams, so that you can attach two separate posters, one looking in one direction and one in another. Also, in most cases you have to provide good illumination for these boards so they can be seen at night. This will involve an additional outlay of capital for fixtures and electricians' labor; the cost will vary depending on how fancy you want to get.

So this is the basic outline for what it takes to get into the large-size billboard business. There are quite a few billboard companies around the country, but in many areas, each virtually has a noncompetitive market. In other words, one operator comes in, sets up several hundred billboards, and because he was there first, nobody else wants to bother to try to give him a run for his money for the local or national advertising dollars.

If you live in a part of the country where the market seems wide open and you have the capital, the time and the interest, I can't think of a better way to make a great deal of money in an overlooked real estate opportunity.

And even if there already is an active billboard company in your area, you would do well to apply the second-look philosophy: Look to see what your competition might be, but then look again to see if there are large areas that aren't covered—or aren't covered *well*—by the existing operator. If you decide you have a good chance to step into a gap in the market, then by all means move on in!

But it's more likely that the average reader of this book would be a little reluctant about making such a big commitment of his time and money to a property ploy with which he probably is unfamiliar. For that reason, I want to focus now in more detail on what I think will be a more manageable concept for most investors: the small-size billboard market.

The Junior Poster Panel Business

If I had to start out now as a beginner in the real estate business, I'd probably begin with the small-size billboards, which are called in the trade junior poster panels. I've made many deals over the past two decades in the large-size billboard business, and now, because of my considerable experience in this field, I don't think twice about launching another venture if the time and place are right.

But if you're just a beginner or are relatively inexperienced in this field, getting into the big-billboard business can be almost like a surgeon trying to take on an extremely difficult operation without working up to it through simpler challenges. There are too many chances of making a wrong move if you don't have a sufficient background, either in surgery or in billboard advertising.

The key thing in being a successful billboard entrepreneur—and turning this overlooked real estate ploy into a fortune—is to make a big splash. But even if you don't have the capital to be a big-time operator with the large-size boards, you can still make a big impact with less risk by using junior panels. It's certainly better to be a big-time operator in small boards than a small-time operator, or a failure, in big boards.

Junior panels consist of fewer sheets of paper, as opposed to the usual twelve sheets that make up the larger billboards. Also, the small posters measure only six feet by twelve feet, or one-quarter of the dimensions of the large-size boards.

As with the large billboards, there are several manufacturers around the country that make the junior panels, and they'll ship them out to you in kit form. For example, two companies that handle these are Formetco, Inc., in Norcross, Georgia, just outside of Atlanta, and the Tiffin Art Metal Company in Tiffin, Ohio.

These kits consist of two steel horizontal faces, measuring three feet by twelve feet each. You attach them together, one on top of the other, to get the full junior-panel face of six feet by twelve feet.

To set them up in the ground, all you need is a four-inch pipe, about twenty feet long with a T-bar arrangement on it, to support the junior-panel facing. About six feet of this pipe is inserted into the ground, with fourteen feet standing free, above ground, to support the billboard. The foundation into which the pipe is inserted will usually be a cement mixture to form a collar around the pole.

One nice thing about these structures, by the way, is that they offer you a high percentage of salvage value. If you decide to shift your junior panel to another location, you just come in with a small crane, lift the entire structure, cement collar and all, out of the ground, knock off the cement, and you're ready to put the billboard down on another plot of ground.

But the greatest financial benefit for the junior panels is their cost. Your total outlay for one junior panel, from purchasing materials, to assembly, to placing it in the ground, should only come to about $300 per face—or perhaps $250 per face if you pitch in and contribute some of the labor yourself. This capital expenditure compares rather well with the $3,000 you would have to fork over to put up one regular-size billboard.

Also, your knowledge of the billboard business doesn't

have to be as technical or sophisticated with these smaller boards; and you can probably get by with just a lease person and a salesperson rather than bothering with all the other office people that a large-size billboard business requires.

One other important cost-cutting feature is that advertisers seldom, if ever, require that these junior panels be illuminated. As a result, you don't have to worry about electrical maintenance, such as going around to inspect them regularly to see that the lights are on and the local kids haven't knocked out any of the bulbs.

The eight-sheet billboards, which we're discussing, are often mounted on the walls of buildings, such as grocery stores, rather than erected from the ground as free-standing structures. These small, wall-based billboards can be highly profitable at a relatively low cost if the entrepreneur picks his market carefully. For example, you might go into one community, build fifty of these and place them all close to local grocery stores. I can assure you that with an array of billboard advertising like this, you would have no trouble at all getting local food wholesalers—and perhaps even national brand companies like General Foods—to buy space from you. Advertisers love this particular approach, which involves exposure of their products, in posters, at the closest point of sale.

So what it all comes down to is that your capital risk is relatively small with these junior panels, especially when you compare them with the large investment required to make a go of it in the large billboard game. Now let me break down the figures for you in a typical example to see just how profitable these junior poster panels can be.

Suppose that you want to build 200 junior poster panels, which will cost you about $60,000 to put into place (200 times $300 per poster face equals $60,000). In an average market, you could expect about $75 per month from advertisers for each poster panel, or a total of $15,000 *a month* on a basic investment of $60,000 ($75 times 200 posters equals $15,000). That works out to $180,000 a year, or annual sales of 300 percent on your investment!

Because of the many tax breaks you would get, including deductions for depreciation of the billboard structures and investment tax credits, most, if not all, of this income should be sheltered from income tax.

But let me make one final, important point about financing these small billboards. If a $60,000 investment seems too steep a risk for you to take, don't abandon the billboard idea out of hand. After all, if you were in the market to buy a house and you found one for $60,000, you'd probably jump at the chance to purchase it because that amount is now lower than the average cost of an American single-family dwelling. With a home, you'd automatically think in terms of financing it, and that's exactly what you should do with a billboard company.

You might throw in $5,000 or $10,000 of your own money and then borrow the rest from a bank. Or you could talk up your idea with friends and relatives and get them to invest with you. Even if you end up having to borrow $30,000 from the bank or another institutional financing source, you'll probably be able to pay them back in a couple of months with the income you'll be generating.

So as you can see, the junior-panel approach is well within the means of almost any middle-income family these days. To get some perspective on just how profitable these junior panels can be, let's now compare them briefly with some income figures for a typical large-size billboard operation. For 200 large-size billboards, you can still make a good deal of money—I wouldn't be in the business otherwise! But the rate of return is likely to be far lower and the initial investment much higher.

The example we were talking about a few pages back provides a good illustration of this point. You'll remember that we estimated it would cost about $3,000 to buy, assemble and erect each large-size billboard, or a total of $600,000 for 200 of these boards. With 200 large billboards—the thirty-sheet variety as opposed to the eight-sheet junior poster panels—you could get an average monthly rent from advertisers of about $160 per face. That would give you a sales income of $32,000 per month on an initial investment of about $600,000, which is still an excellent return. It amounts to $384,000, or about 64 percent annual sales on your $600,000 investment. The operating profit could be 25 percent of sales. But at the same time, these large-size billboards, as good as they are, offer a considerably lower return than what you can expect on the junior panels, even if most of the income is sheltered from income taxes.

At this point you may be wondering, "Why is Dooner in the large-size billboard business at all, if the junior poster panels are so much more profitable?" There are several reasons. In the first place, for a big operator, you have much more flexibility with the large boards. Most advertisers, especially national advertisers, prefer to use more big boards than junior posters simply because they make a bigger visual impact. Also, even though I've quoted some average figures above for the large boards, there's no reason for you to assume that all billboard businesses must operate at that average. I usually try to establish billboard companies that are going to function with higher rents or lower costs than the ones I've quoted, and in most cases, I've managed to succeed with this objective.

So these are some of my reasons for sticking with the

big billboards. But for most people, especially those with no experience in the advertising field and limited capital, I would recommend the junior poster panels. And when you get one junior poster operation set up and it begins to turn a profit (a tax-sheltered profit!), that's just the beginning. You'll always be looking for more space for more boards, and you'll constantly be finding it.

It's amazing to me how billboard opportunities just appear, almost like magic, before my eyes as I drive around in almost any part of the country. The main reason that I see these possibilities is that I'm conditioned to study every interesting situation closely, to always take that second look. And when I combine this tendency with the fact that I have a lot of experience with billboards, the process of making money in this field of overlooked real estate becomes almost too easy! Uninviting blank walls or neglected, overgrown strips of land near roadways suddenly begin to beckon like a bankbook.

But those are reactions that I've built up for about twenty-five years in the business. If you don't have that sort of background with billboards, you first have to learn a few marketing techniques and begin to apply them in some practical situations. Eventually, your reactions in this particular field of real estate will become developed well enough to allow you to perceive an overlooked rags-to-riches opportunity almost instinctively, without having to think too hard about it.

One of the ways you can develop a proper "feel" for this type of real estate investment is to learn what is required of one good billboard—and, by natural projection, of a good billboard market. And to learn this skill, it's necessary to find out what the potential is for billboard advertising in your community and then get out on the streets and roads in your area and try your hand at picking likely spots to place your junior posters.

Here are a few practical steps to get you started in the junior poster panel field:

Step One: Check your local zoning codes.

This is a fairly simple procedure but an extremely important one. What you're trying to find out here is whether or not you can erect billboards in your community at all, and, if you can, whether or not there are restrictions on the locations.

You can hire a lawyer to check this out for you, or if you've hooked up with a partner who knows the ropes about billboard operations, that may be even better. He may be able to get on the phone and give you an answer to your zoning questions in a half-hour or less.

If you don't have a knowledgeable operations person and don't want to go through the expense and time of hiring a lawyer, you may just want to check the zoning codes out by yourself. It's not hard: You just go down to the local government's building office, find a helpful clerk and get him to steer you to a copy of the local code book, which is available for every single incorporated community in the United States.

You can find the zoning regulations you're looking for by checking in the code index under a heading such as "billboards" or "signs." The regulations will likely say something like, "Signs exceeding 120 square feet are not permitted in the area zoned . . ."

Keep in mind while you're looking through the regulations that the junior panels are only six by twelve feet, or seventy-two square feet. So even if there are severe restrictions on the size of the signs permitted in your community, you'll probably still find that the standard junior poster panels qualify. There will be a tremendous market for these smaller billboards in those communities where the larger signs are prohibited.

Step Two: Get traffic-count maps for your area.

After checking the zoning regulations, the very next thing that a prospective billboard investor should do— before spending a dime on another thing—is to obtain maps of his city or region with traffic counts listed on them. These maps, which are usually available from one of the city offices, a local traffic audit bureau or the state highway department, may seem to be quite boring at first blush. But you'll find them to be invaluable when you begin to look for possible lease locations and to make a sales pitch to possible advertisers.

These traffic-flow maps, as they're sometimes called, show the average traffic per day on various roads in your area. These figures are generally accepted as being valid by advertisers and are usually thought to represent, within 5 percent accuracy, the actual traffic in a region.

So before you or your lease person starts scouting out possible locations for billboards, it's smart to check your traffic-flow map and see which streets and highways you should concentrate on. When you finally pick your locations and line up your leases, these maps can then be used as part of a sales presentation to local and national advertisers.

For example, if you tell an advertising prospect that a particular sign is going to cost him $300 a month, you can show him at the same time that, according to the traffic counts for that area, he'll get an exposure of 40,000 people each day among the motorists who will drive past the sign. That will amount to only about 25 cents a day for each thousand people he can reach with your sign—a pretty convincing argument, I'd say, when compared with prices for TV spots or newspaper ads.

Step Three: Secure the required permits and leases you'll need to operate a billboard company in your locality.

These will probably include a business license that identifies you as an outdoor advertising operator and a building permit, so that you can legally build, paint and erect the required billboard structures.

Step Four: Find some good partners.

If you have no experience in the industry, it will be extremely helpful, if not essential, for you to bring in as a partner someone who knows the billboard business, or at least something about advertising. You should do plenty of homework on billboard investing before you start making contacts with any prospective employees or partners. It's easy to do a snow job on somebody with just a little bit of knowledge in this industry, so you have to be sure you know a little more than the average guy who is adept at selling himself with a glib sales line. For example, it would be a good idea to get a list of your prospective partner's contacts and references and then check a few of them to be sure that he's telling you the truth about his credentials in the industry.

After you've chosen a likely partner, what kind of a deal should you set up with him? Since the original idea and possibly most of the capital is coming from you, you should definitely keep a majority interest in the business. In fact, I would recommend that you try to limit your partner's interest to no more than 25 percent of the company unless he's going to be contributing a significant amount of money himself. One reason you want to keep as much ownership of the company as you can is that you may soon find you want to bring in additional partners or shareholders. For example, you might want to include a person who has a lot of money to invest for further expansion or someone who has special expertise in the billboard business that neither you nor your first partner can provide.

But there are also countervailing considerations that you should keep in mind to be sure you don't dole out too small a percentage of the company. For example, if you drive too hard a bargain and your associate receives too small a piece of the action, he may become resentful in your future relationships with him. Remember: You have to work with this guy, so do all you can to keep him happy in the financial arrangements!

Also, it's easy for a person with little or no percentage to begin to feel, after the business is going, "Gee, I do all the work, and he gets all the money." That sort of attitude can only hurt the productivity of your enterprise and undercut the profits that you both hope to make. So it's better to give a little more to your associate and ensure that he'll have an incentive to put out his best efforts.

Of course, there are many other ways to give a person a piece of the action without actually giving a percentage of the equity of the company. For example, you might pay your lease person a salary of $15,000 to $18,000 a year and on top of that give him or her some sort of commission on each space sale or lead. Or the person could be paid so much of a bonus for every lease that is signed in excess of ten sites per month.

Some owners have it worked out so that they can afford to pay $100 a year per face on each of their billboard sites. Then, if their lease person goes out and negotiates a lease for $50 a year, the owner may give him a bonus equal to the balance that he had *expected* to pay, or $50. Even by paying the $50 difference as a bonus here, the owner ultimately comes out well ahead, because he will probably be paying the $50 rate or something close to it for years, but he only has to pay the bonus once. And the bonus has probably operated as a powerful incentive to prompt the lease person to drive a tougher bargain to secure as low a lease rate as he possibly could.

So, to carry this example to its conclusion, if the owner continued to pay the $50 lease amount for five years, that would be a total of $250 in lease expenses. In contrast, if he had paid what the going rate was ($100 a year), he would have paid twice as much, or $500. By giving his lease person that $50 bonus as an incentive, he upped his five-year expenses to $300, but that's still considerably lower than the $500 he might have had to pay if the lease person had failed to drive a hard bargain with the property owner.

But lease men or women aren't the only ones who can be provided with an incentive in this way. Take the salesperson, for example. Her salary is always negotiable, and it can be linked with a commission of as much as 10 percent of each sale if she makes a national sale or 20 percent if the sale is to a local company.

But there is still likely to come a time when this sales or lease person, if she's really good, will say to you, "Look,

I don't mind working for you and building this business, but I'd like an option right now to buy some of the company—because even though you've put up the money, I've got some important experience to offer in the future." And it may well make sense at that time to offer her a percentage of your own holdings to give her even more of a stake in the future of the company.

Step Five: Pick some billboard locations and get leases on them.

Picking a good billboard location is largely a matter of common sense. The key principle is that the billboard, whether it's a large-size one or a junior poster panel, should offer maximum visibility to motorists or pedestrians moving at their average rate of speed along the adjacent roadway or walkway.

As a rule of thumb, I usually figure that I need at least 250 feet or more of uninterrupted approach for a large billboard and at least fifty to seventy-five feet for a smaller, junior poster panel. The junior panels may be as suitable for pedestrians or motorists, depending on where you set them up, but I'd still go for at least fifty feet of uninterrupted approach space for them.

But it's unwise to try to abide rigidly by any abstract formula here. If you have 250 feet, but for some reason the practical, physical surroundings of the location still make it difficult to see or read your sign, then you have to throw the formula out and focus more on the actual layout of the location.

In any case, I would advise you to get a couple of associates to stand at the exact spot where you want to build the billboard and have them hold a couple of poles with highly visible little flags. The poles should be connected by a piece of gauze or tape the exact length of your proposed billboard.

Then they should stand with the tape held taut and the poles held precisely vertical so that you can see exactly how the billboard will fit into the space you're considering. Have your associates move forward and backward and shift the angles at which they stand. When they are in just the right position, signal to them, and then drive some stakes into the spots where they are standing so that you'll know just where to position your billboard.

With the junior poster panels, you may not have as good a shot at getting a huge number of big national advertisers as with the large-size boards. But in many ways, the smaller billboards can offer more flexibility in terms of location.

For example, many shopping centers don't like to have the big billboards because they can overwhelm the property too much. But there are many places in these centers that would be possibilities for the junior poster panels. So be creative and flexible in your thinking when you're looking for locations. The fact that you're new at the game may well work to your advantage because you won't be hampered by traditional preconceptions about where a "proper" billboard should be placed.

Once you've chosen your location, then the time has arrived to nail down your lease. You may want to lease the property outright for several years if you have already received a definite commitment from an advertiser. As I've already indicated, at the time of the writing of this book a yearly lease payment of about $100 would be appropriate for a junior poster panel location. But you may be able to pay less or you may want to pay more, depending on what you can negotiate with the landowner and how much your advertiser is willing to pay you. In any case, a single structure averages $50 per year per face (or $100 for a two-face billboard). It's the per-face average that really counts since sales are projected on the basis of "faces" for sale, not sites.

Finally, if you haven't gotten a commitment yet from an advertiser, you might try buying an *option* to lease from the landowner for a smaller amount than what he's asking for a yearly lease. In this way, you can tie up the property for a couple of months to give yourself enough time to sell the space to an advertiser.

Step Six: Sell your billboard space to advertisers.

Nobody is going to beat down your door in an effort to buy billboard space from you, especially if you're new to the business, unless you're out there pushing. You've got to sell the space *actively,* and the best way to do that is to be pleasantly aggressive and innovative.

One effective selling concept I came up with was to find a location I liked and then buy a sixty-day option to rent the property. In most parts of the country, except some of the densely populated big cities, you can buy an option like this for just a few dollars. Since the actual lease on a junior poster panel might cost only about $100 a year, you can see that an option for a couple of months could be little more than pocket change.

After I had the option, I would take a photograph of the property—either the specific plot of ground or the roof of the building where I was planning on placing my billboard—at the spot and angle from which motorists would likely see it. Then I'd cut a piece out of the eight-by-ten photo at the same place and in the same size and proportion as the billboard I expected to place there. And I'd put a bright-colored piece of paper behind that spot on the photo so that the proposed billboard location would really stand out.

Then, I'd take this rather impressive graphic display and my traffic-flow maps to prospective advertisers, and I'd make a strong argument to them to the effect that by buying my billboard space they could reach a such-and-such number of people on that particular route each day. And in plenty of cases, right from the very beginning of my career in real estate, they have been interested enough to sign up with me.

Another rather innovative sales technique that has worked for me has been to use a rotation method on my billboards so that by signing up with me an advertiser can often get a much wider coverage than if he just rented one billboard in one fixed location.

For example, I worked out a deal in the Fox River Valley of Wisconsin where I rotated about ten billboards this way. I found a high location with excellent visibility in several heavy-traffic towns and then put up my billboard structures. But then I rotated each of those ten billboards every sixty days so that my clients reached an entirely new town at each two-month interval.

Each of the billboard structures in the various towns had exactly the same-size frame, so all I needed to do was take the billboard from Green Bay, let's say, and sixty days later remove its face and bring that to Appleton. At the same time, I'd transfer the face from Appleton to another market, and so on, all through that particular region.

In this way, even though I was new to the area, I immediately caught the attention of the regional advertisers because they knew that for the first time they could get coverage in a much larger group of markets—by paying the same amount of money each month.

As you line up your advertisers, you'll probably find that if you're setting up your billboard real estate venture in one of the top twenty-five urban markets in the United States, about 80 percent of your advertising could come from national advertisers—companies that produce automobiles, national-brand foods, liquor and cigarettes.

If you're in a smaller town, of say about 50,000 people, you'll probably find that 40 percent of your business is still national. But the other 60 percent will be from local businesses—funeral parlors, restaurants and savings and loan associations. There won't be much problem getting the posters for the national advertisers because most of them have their own in-house advertising departments or work through agencies that provide standard graphic materials.

But your local customers may well require creative help, as they are not often represented by an advertising agency. Most of them will probably know less about advertising and graphics than you do, and so you'll have to help them put together the sales copy and design that will get their messages across on your billboard.

For example, if you contact a local savings and loan association, they may be willing to buy space on five of your boards each month for a year. They may also have a vague idea of what they want to say, such as putting their logo on the board and some message about second mortgages they're offering. But it will be up to you to take all that information and get it put together for them in an artistically acceptable form.

One way to go about this is to hire a freelance artist to do a rough sketch, which can then be sent back to the advertisers for their approval. When their approval is obtained, the artist will then work the layout up into final copy that a printer can make into a billboard poster. The artist should be especially familiar with outdoor advertising layouts. Frequently, this person can be found on the payroll of one of the leading local advertising companies, and he or she may be willing to "moonlight" a sketch for you for perhaps $50 to $200.

In many cases, the printing company you plan to use will provide their own art department and they may be able to do the preliminary artwork for you at a lower cost, say about $25 to $50. This price may well be less than you could get from a free-lancer or a design company that specializes in layouts of this type. But you'll have to shop around in your area to find the best price—as well as the most competent work.

Remember: As with other types of businesses, you don't want to skimp on quality just to get the lowest price. If you use an artist whose posters look amateurish or a printer who does inferior work, you'll probably lose your advertiser and also hurt your reputation as a billboard operator in your community.

As you set up these deals with your advertisers, it's also important to keep in mind the wear and tear that will inevitably occur with your posters. Billboard paper will ride on a poster panel for a good sixty days without getting torn up or messy-looking. So you should figure that, with our savings and loan example described above, five posters on five different billboards will last for about two months before you have to replace them. Therefore, you might suggest that your customer put a different message on the panels after sixty days and then perhaps return to the original message sixty days after that, or maybe even at the same time the following year if the design is seasonal.

But keep in mind, before you change your style of posters too often, that it's cheaper to use the same poster concept over and over. The reason for this is that even though you have to run off a new set of posters every sixty days, you *don't* have to go through an entirely different set of artistic and production procedures.

Also, it's much cheaper, if you can plan out one advertiser's billboard schedule for an entire year, to run off all the posters that you expect to use during the year at the same time. Then you would store them in a safe place and use them as the need arises. By the "economies of size," you should save a good deal of money this way because your costs in producing each unit of printed matter will almost always go down as the total amount of your production goes up. Conversely, if you have to go through arranging the artwork and printing up an entirely different set of posters every sixty days, your costs of production will be higher.

Now, let's put all this on a dollars-and-cents basis. If the savings and loan association wants to rent five junior poster panels a month from you for an entire year, and it wants only two sets of poster designs, which will be alternated every sixty days, then you would need to order fifteen posters of each design, or a total of thirty posters, to cover the entire year.

If you charge the client $75 per face for space, that would amount to a monthly charge of $375. And the posters might cost an average of about $20 apiece in printing expenses, or a total one-time charge of $600 for the thirty posters you need.

In contrast, if the account decided it wanted twelve different designs during the year, with a different advertising message each month, instead of the two designs that we've assumed in our example, the cost of production would soar—perhaps up to $100 a month or more, or a total yearly expenditure of $1,200.

As with any other product that you might want to sell, real estate such as billboards can be peddled through a variety of promotional techniques. For example, if the advertiser agrees to buy the space for a full year, you might offer him as an incentive a 10 percent discount. Providing special deals and discounts like this is always worth it to you because that way you'll (1) decrease your vacant space over the course of a year, and (2) reduce your sales costs if you can secure a twelve-month noncancelable contract.

Step Seven: Organize your paperwork carefully.

There needn't be much paperwork involved in a billboard venture, but what there is should be organized carefully because you'll find yourself dealing with a number of important legal documents.

For one thing, you should secure a *noncompeting agreement* from any partners you bring into the business with you. Otherwise, they may learn a great deal working with you, make a lot of contacts, and then proceed to start up their own competing business and take some of your clients away. Your attorney can help you draw up a simple contract along these lines.

In addition, you'll need a *lease form* for the landowners you sign up for your billboard leases. This document should be relatively short and simple because too often a very lengthy document will scare away landowners who are not accustomed to dealing regularly in real estate transactions. On the other hand, there are certain key clauses that should be included just to protect your interests.

Typically, the lease form is a six-by-eight-inch sheet of paper with your company's name at the top. It states that the agreement is between your company and a certain landowner, who represents either himself or his company as the owner and lessor. Then the agreement says that for a certain sum of dollars per year (or month) you have permission to erect a billboard structure of a certain description on his property. You will also have open access to that structure during the period of the lease.

Finally, there should be some sort of provision to the effect that if the owner sells his building or land, you'll agree to remove your poster panel from his property within, say, sixty days of his written notice to you.

Many forms of this type are available around the industry, and you may also get some leads either from the national trade association, the Institute of Outdoor Advertising, or from the trade publication, *Signs of the Times,* which you can find out about from your local library. In any case, I'd be sure to keep this document simple and have it printed in relatively large letters so that it will be easy for your lessors to understand—and thus less likely to scare them away from entering into a deal with you.

Finally, another form that you'll need in your business is a *display contract,* which is used to lay out your agreement with your advertisers. In this document you agree to sell a certain designated billboard space at a certain location to a particular advertiser. He, in turn, contracts to rent the space from you at a certain price for a specified period of time. This is another form that's widely available in the industry, or you can have your attorney draft up your own special version if you like.

Step Eight: Stagger your lease schedules.

Whenever you're using real estate as a base to operate a property-oriented business, it's important to pay close attention to maintaining a steady cash flow. One way to help achieve this goal is to schedule your lease payments so that they don't all come due at the same time. When you're first setting up shop and your initial leases start coming in, there may be a temptation to pay all of them up front. For example, you may decide that doing this will make your bookkeeping simpler so that you won't have to keep track of monthly or quarterly payments.

But if you start dealing with hundreds or even thousands of leases, you'll find that the lease payments, even though they are individually small, can amount to a great deal of money if they are all lumped together. So it's easiest on your pocket to stretch out the payments you have to make to various landowners. For example, instead of paying $200 in advance to an owner, you might pay just $50 in advance per quarter. In this way, you'd have the use of your money over the entire year, and you may well need that money to meet payroll expenses or pay for your own food and rent!

Step Nine: Get totally involved with your billboards, from start to finish.

All good entrepreneurs know that no successful business just runs by itself, and billboards are certainly no exception to this rule. You can't treat any rags-to-riches real estate project as a passive investment, and you have to be especially active in a venture like billboards.

By getting involved in the business, you'll learn through experience how to confront a variety of problems as they occur and also how to overcome those problems and prevent them from happening again. By being involved in the nuts and bolts of your business, you'll also be more visible to other business people in the community. As a result, you'll meet more important contacts and be in a position to take advantage of new opportunities when they occur later.

So if you decide to try your hand at this overlooked property investment opportunity, immerse yourself in it! That's the only way you'll know you've given yourself every chance to make a go of it—and perhaps even achieve an extraordinary success as a real estate investor in your community.

These, then, are some practical guidelines for becoming a successful investor in the billboard aspect of the real estate business. But now let me use a rather exciting example from my own experience to show you something more about overlooked real estate that has implications that go far beyond the billboard business.

8

Take a Second Look at the Competition

MANY TIMES, while you're looking around for depressed, neglected or overlooked real estate opportunities, you may stumble upon what at first seems a property concept that has tremendous profit potential. But then you may see that even if you build up that overlooked piece of property, you're going to run head-on into tremendous competition from some other operator in the market.

You'll recall that I learned some important things about competition in business when I was just a kid peddling newspapers and other small items on the streets of New York City. I usually tried to work parts of the city that were virgin territory, without any direct competitors. But sometimes that just wasn't possible. Sometimes if I started in a good area without any other young salesmen around, somebody would get wind of my success and start to try to move in and push me out.

In those days I learned that in most cases I eventually had to take a stand—even if it meant getting into a fistfight—and defend the business territory I had worked so hard to cultivate. As an adult in real estate investment,

I of course don't resort to violence to deal with my competitors. But many of the same principles of dealing with
competition that I learned as a kid still apply.

First of all, if you hope to be successful in rags-to-riches
real estate investments, you can't turn tail and run every
time a competitor appears on the horizon. As a matter of
fact, if you're onto something profitable and exciting, you
should *expect* to have to deal with competitors before
long. Their entry onto the field of property combat just
confirms the fact that you're on the right track. Besides,
if you got there first, you're probably going to stay ahead
of them if you just refuse to panic and keep doing what
you're doing.

In the second place, *all* successful real estate investment must eventually become competitive. By definition,
what the successful investor wants to create is a piece of
property or a property concept that will attract as many
investor dollars as possible from the limited pool of money
that people have to put into things other than their daily
living expenses.

For example, there are many people who would like
to sell their homes right now, but for a number of reasons
—especially the unavailability of good financing—there
aren't too many viable buyers. So if you're trying to sell
your home, you're in an extremely competitive real estate
situation, but it's a situation that shouldn't necessarily dis-
courage you from trying to find a buyer. Instead, the competitive atmosphere should prompt you to think more
creatively and act more aggressively in convincing some
of those people in the limited group of buyers you encounter that the home you have to offer is better than
anyone else's.

In this regard, I'm reminded of an article in a recent
issue of *Forbes* that recommended that people who want
to make their homes stand out favorably from those off-

ered by other would-be sellers should concentrate especially on remodeling their kitchens. It seems that more
informal entertaining and more family interaction are
taking place there than in the past. As a result, homemak-
ers, consciously or subconsciously, are often swayed by
the look and utility value of a kitchen more than they are
by any other part of the house.

Also, if you're a homeowner who wants to sell in a
competitive market, it can be very helpful to learn more
about creative methods of financing a home, so that more
of your prospective buyers will be able to swing the sale.
For example, you might take on a second mortgage at a
relatively low interest rate and thus help out a buyer who
may have trouble paying a bank at much higher interest
rates.

I learned the rudiments of this principle when I was
out on the New York streets as a kid selling those almost-
wilting flowers that I told you about in the first chapter.
I was able to buy the flowers at a low rate from a Greek
flower shop on Saturday afternoons because they were too
far gone to be refrigerated over the weekends. Then I got
out on the sidewalks just as the movie and theater crowds
were beginning to arrive and was successful in competing
with dozens of local flower shops. Why? Because what I
was offering was (1) immediately available, in that people
could get them on the street rather than going into a shop,
and (2) far less expensive than the fresher flowers carried
by the regular florists.

The third and final principle I've learned over the
years about competition is that it's often a good idea to
consider jumping directly into a competitive situation
when you encounter it. Listen closely to what I'm saying
because it may sound slightly insane at first: *You should
examine every competitive real estate situation very closely to see whether or not it may be hiding a property ploy*

or overlooked real estate opportunity that you can exploit profitably.

Now, I realize this principle I'm stating may run counter to everything you've ever heard about investing successfully in real estate—or becoming successful in any sort of business, for that matter. But think about it for a moment: It just makes sense, doesn't it, that most really lucrative property situations have already been discovered and are in the process of being exploited by somebody? Yet in most cases I have found that those profit centers have only been *partially* used to the best advantage. In other words, there are always many possible variations for transforming any given piece of neglected or overlooked property into a fortune. And the successful person you're observing in a particular market has found one, but *only* one, of those ways.

So apply the second-look philosophy to competitive real estate situations you encounter as well as to property that may be lying isolated, neglected or fallow. There may be a number of holes in the competition where you can make your mark—and make a nice profit in the process.

One of the best illustrations I've encountered of hidden opportunity in intense real estate competition involved a billboard venture I started in Atlanta. But the implications and lessons of that experience go far beyond the billboard business. At first, if you're a person with only modest means and little experience in high-powered real estate dealings, you may wonder, "What does a deal like this have to teach me?" But I think you'll see that many of the elements in this situation can have a direct application to you, no matter what kind of overlooked property investment you may be considering now or may confront in the future.

This story begins in late 1976, when my wife, Ellie, our five children and I moved to Atlanta from Ireland, where we had made our home for a few years. Actually, Ellie and the kids had been spending much more time in Ireland than I had. I had been on the go constantly for a long time, traveling back and forth across the Atlantic to attend to my real estate interests in the United States. But there just seemed to be too much hectic activity in my life and too many separations from my family. So I decided I'd like to slow down a bit, perhaps get out of some of the real estate businesses that I didn't really enjoy that much, and pay more attention to those that I did like.

We picked Atlanta because several business colleagues who lived there had been encouraging me to try life in that part of the South. Also, the city was central to a number of the businesses I had going at the time. You'll remember that during this period I had bought and was in the process of building up those depressed, over-the-hill motels that Holiday Inn had sold me in Hattiesburg, Mississippi, Houston, Texas, and Oak Ridge, Tennessee.

Atlanta, with its central location and ready access through airplane flights to these properties, seemed an ideal location. Also, I had easy access to Indianapolis and the billboard companies I owned in that vicinity and to St. Louis, which was close to where my Hen House restaurants were headquartered. I could take a plane to those cities, visit my real estate holdings and be back the same night if I wanted to make a quick trip.

When I first moved to Atlanta, I didn't have any particular thoughts about getting into any real estate ventures there. But I naturally started noticing the outdoor advertising that was available in the area, mainly because I had been conditioned through my own billboard interests to always keep my eyes open. I was particularly intrigued by the fact that all the signs seemed to bear the imprint "Turner" at the bottom of the billboard.

I'd known of the Turner billboard organization for

some years. It's a big outfit and at the time was the only poster advertiser in Atlanta. The owner, Ted Turner, is known all over the country for his activities in cable television and as the owner of several professional sports organizations, including the Atlanta Braves baseball team.

My personal impression of Turner was, and still is, quite positive. He's a man who seems to be always on the cutting edge of every field he enters. In many ventures he's years ahead of his time—so far ahead sometimes that he's forced to bide his time until everyone else catches up. As the founder of television's Cable News Network and as an experimenter with many special market concepts on cable TV, he sometimes seems to be overreaching himself. But I believe that his vision of the future direction of the mass media is generally correct and that the pioneering efforts he's making today will eventually bear significant fruit.

So in every sense of the term, Ted Turner was a real "high-wire act" in Atlanta, even at the time that I arrived there. He was always trying risky new ventures and more often than not was succeeding at them, as ordinary folks watched breathlessly from the sidelines.

The common reaction to anyone who was considering competing with Turner in any of his many fields of expertise was: "Too bad for that guy! You can't win against Turner! He's got too much money, too much creativity, too much luck, etc., etc."

But when I started hearing comments like that, my ears perked up. I knew enough about the opportunities, especially the real estate opportunities, that often lay between the cracks of intense competition to understand that Atlanta might offer some great advertising possibilities for me as well.

Since I was in the process of freeing myself from some

other business commitments, I saw that I would soon have some capital to invest in a venture somewhere. And Atlanta began to look more and more inviting and exciting, especially since the only billboard company in town was owned by this charismatic operator whom I was willing to test on the field of real estate competition.

In scouting the Atlanta market, I noticed from the imprint on certain signs that a junior poster panel operator named Reese was also in the business. He had a number of these panels around town, about 180 or so, and had managed to secure a couple of major national advertisers as clients. It was this Reese, I decided, who could be my key to the Atlanta market. He'd obviously been in the city for a while and he would know something about the Turner organization; and also he probably had contacts with many important advertisers.

I never beat around the bush in a situation like this. I don't try to find mutual friends to introduce me or soften a guy up with a lot of introductory letters. I just picked up the phone and dialed him directly. As it turned out, Lawrence Reese was the salesman, lease man, manager, owner, president and everything else in his company. We immediately established a rapport: I could tell by the way we related in that phone conversation that we were going to hit it off.

So I suggested that we get together and talk about a business deal the two of us might be able to put together, and he seemed willing to give me a hearing. That's something else for anybody interested in real estate investment to keep in mind. Don't be shy about listening to people who come to you with a new property ploy!

Obviously, if you become reasonably successful, an increasing number of people are going to start beating a path to your door with venture ideas. In most cases you'll probably want to send them gently on their way. But sometimes a guy is going to ring you up with a dynamite idea that could totally change your life and set you up to make a fortune. So don't reject anyone or any proposal out of hand. Listen, evaluate and ponder carefully first; *then* make your decision.

Reese didn't know me at all. Here I was, a total stranger calling him out of left field and suggesting a business meeting. He could easily have said, "Sorry, I haven't the time. Send me a letter."

But he wasn't that sort of person. He was open to new concepts and wanted very much to expand his operations. When we met, my initial positive impression of him was confirmed. He was a rather quiet guy and that complemented my own Irish loquacity very nicely, and so we got along well from the start.

I had learned from some personal research I had done before our meeting that he was well liked by a lot of the business people in the community. Some of the advertising executives and building inspectors were especially drawn to him. Apparently, he was viewed as something of an underdog since he was the lone David competing against the Goliath Turner organization.

As a matter of fact, he had been employed twice by Turner Advertising, but he had had some sort of falling out with their management. As a result, he went into competition with them by using junior panels, which weren't really Turner's specialty. But his problem was that he wasn't too well capitalized: Much of his money was borrowed, and he was forever paying back loans.

As we talked, I asked him a few key questions about his assessment of the Atlanta market: "What about the large billboard situation? Is there a possibility of building a competitive billboard company?"

Of course, he knew exactly what I meant. He was a savvy guy, and he immediately saw that I was probing to see if we might be able to combine our forces as partners. He said he thought there was room for another company, but he stressed it would take a lot of work.

So I said, "Well, what about these junior panels you have? Can we convert some of them over? Could we just take down the small signs and go ahead and build some of the big ones on some of the same properties?"

He said he figured that maybe sixty could be converted to the big boards. And as we talked further, we both realized that this idea of converting some of the junior panel sites to large-size billboards would be a fine way to start. Here was the beginning of a property ploy that had a good chance to work.

We couldn't move ahead with the deal just then, however. I was in the process of selling my hotels in Houston and Hattiesburg, and I was also mulling over the idea of unloading my billboard companies in Indiana and Illinois. I knew that while I still had those ventures on my mind, I couldn't focus enough of my attention on the situation in Atlanta. Also, I needed some capital from the sale of those holdings to give me a strong financial base in the Atlanta market.

So Reese and I put our discussions on hold for a while. And here's another lesson for the beginning real estate investor: Sometimes it's wise to let a new idea simmer for a while before you make a big commitment of your time or money.

Of course, an opportunity may present itself and you have to move quickly to take advantage of it. But more often you'll have a few weeks or months—or even years— to turn a concept over in your mind and fine-tune it in discussions with trusted associates. The most successful ventures are those that you've planned thoroughly in advance and that have all the wrinkles ironed out before you risk your time and money.

Reese was a total real estate professional in this regard, because he was very patient and didn't push me. I suppose he needed to do some thinking, just as I did. We both knew that here was the possibility of moving into a market successfully against an established giant, and we didn't want to blow it by making any stupid mistakes or false moves.

We realized that we couldn't just put up a few billboards and hope for the best. With Turner Advertising as a competitor, everything had to be worked out like clockwork, with things ready to be set in motion just as we needed them to happen. For example, we needed site leases—lots of them—and also advertisers ready and waiting in the wings as the billboards went up.

Most important of all, we had to think through all the contingencies and plan *each step* we would take as we built up our billboard challenge to Turner. At the same time, we had to *anticipate* how the competition would react and then plan our countermoves. It's important in a situation like this to always stay on the offensive, always have an aggressive response for every action your competitor takes against you. It also was extremely important that all our strategies and tactics be kept *undercover*. We couldn't afford to alert the competition about what we were up to at this early stage of the game.

Of course, it's possible to step over the line and get involved either in unfair or even illegal tactics against your opponents. And I firmly believe that's absolutely wrong. But the kind of competition I'm describing here is much closer to a championship athletic contest. You have two teams, one pitted against the other in direct, one-on-one competition for the top prize.

The teams don't disclose their pregame tactics to each other. They plan and practice their approach in private and then spring as many surprises on their opponents as they can in their effort to win the championship. And if both teams play well, then both, in a sense, win. Only one may end up in first place, but both are still at the top of their league and they will both be back next year to test their mettle against each other once more.

If you hope to find and exploit overlooked property investment opportunities successfully in a hotly contested market, you have to assume this attitude. You have to decide you're going to plunge right into the competition and *enjoy* yourself in the excitement of the struggle. In the last analysis, there's really no reason to be afraid of a big operator. He probably doesn't have time to concentrate on the specific challenge you've decided to make against his market, and he may be an easier mark than the other little guy who is holding on to his more limited amount of business turf for dear life.

But now, back to our story. Finally, the time arrived to form the company. It was the summer of 1978, about two years after Reese and I had had our first meeting. I arranged to buy his company in return for his receiving cash and some stock in the new company we were to form—Reese Outdoor Advertising (later changed to Atlanta Outdoor Advertising).

Several other investors and I then got together and sliced up the rest of the ownership of the company in return for some loans and cash investments for shares. These were funds in addition to the loan that we obtained from the C & S Bank in Atlanta. In return for their cash investments, my investors received an option to buy, at $10 a share, stock in the company in proportion to the amount of the notes they had put up.

I acquired 70 percent of the outstanding stock for $35,000. The rest of the stock was sold to the investors for $15,000, which represented approximately 30 percent of the ownership. The total common stock of the company amounted to $50,000 for 5,000 shares. In addition, the investors put in a total of $279,000 in notes which did not have to be repaid for five years. We then went to the C & S Bank with our notes in hand to show them that we had "blood in the deal"—or that we believed enough in what we were doing to put a significant amount of our own money on the line. And the bank granted us a loan of $500,000, to be repaid over five years.

Since billboard companies are so few and therefore not very well known to the banking community, we were very fortunate to meet a young vice president named Don Leslie at C & S. Although our loan proposal had already been rejected by two other major Atlanta banks, Don insisted on a further look. He phoned our references, called our prospective advertisers and even "rode" the sites we had leased and inspected our construction. He is one of the finest, most thorough bankers I've ever met, and finally, when he had decided we passed muster, he approved the loan.

These financial arrangements and negotiations are typical of many of the deals I put together for all sorts of real estate ventures. You have to have a reasonable amount of private money to convince a bank to back you. So you get a group of friends and acquaintances to go in with you as investors. They lend the corporation some money at a decent interest rate—though one *below* what the bank would charge. And then this loan gives them the right to buy some stock in the company. It's their equity ownership, through the stock, that gives them the chance to make some real money on the deal.

For example, if one of my billboard deals is successful, a $10 share of stock might easily be worth $500 or $1,000 in a year or two. So if a person puts in $15,000 in notes and thus qualifies for 20 shares of stock at $10 a share (or a total of $200 worth of stock), he or she might well walk away with stock worth $10,000 when the company has been built up and perhaps sold out in a couple of years. This gain, by the way, would be *in addition to* having received interest on his loan and also having the principal of the loan returned in full after the company has been sold.

After we had assembled our investors and nailed down our financing, we began to plan our strategy in more detail. And it was during this period that an incident occurred that I've since come to regard as almost eerie. Ellie and I were invited to a basketball game with a friend of ours and his wife, and after the contest was over, who should appear on the other side of the court and start walking toward us but Ted Turner.

I had met Ted once before, years ago at a meeting of some billboard entrepreneurs in Wisconsin. It was just a "hello" type of encounter, and then we each went off in opposite directions to spend time with other people. I remembered him, in part because I had read about him in the newspapers since our initial encounter. But I doubted he would remember me.

As it happened that night in Atlanta, he was walking over to say hello to the very man who had invited us to the basketball game. When he arrived on our side of the court, my friend said, "Ted, this is a friend of mine, Bill Dooner. He just moved to Atlanta."

It was a strange kind of meeting. Turner hesitated for a moment and there seemed to be a flash of recognition that passed across his face. And he said, "Oh," as though he did recognize me or felt he should know who I was.

But it was obvious as my host continued, that Turner didn't quite connect with my identity. "Bill is in the same business you're in, Ted," my friend said.

"What business is that?" Turner asked. He had so many businesses that I suppose he probably identified with a different one every hour of the day. Yet at that moment I had a sense that he knew exactly what business I was in.

"I'm in the outdoor business," I said.

He looked hard at me again and said, "Oh. Well, what are you going to do in Atlanta?"

"I'm just looking around," I said. And that was entirely accurate. I was just looking around. But what I didn't tell him was that I might be looking at a virtual skyline of Dooner billboards within a year's time.

I was fairly certain after Turner had left us that evening that he didn't know who I was, and I was hoping to stay in the background of the Atlanta business scene for as long as possible. We were convinced of the necessity of the element of surprise in our project, and so, for example, it was no accident that we named our new company Reese Outdoor Advertising. The theory behind this was that even if the Turner people found out that their old colleague Reese was thinking of putting up a few billboards here and there, they probably wouldn't think twice about it. They wouldn't suspect that Reese now had considerable financial backing that would enable him to launch a full-scale challenge against Turner Advertising.

But despite the thorough planning we had done and the solid financing we had secured, we still had plenty of work ahead of us before we erected our first billboard. We had to evaluate everything about the Atlanta market and how Turner's organization was exploiting it.

The key thing about taking a second look at the competition is to see those areas where they are not operating at all or at least where they are not operating well. Then, when you identify these neglected or overlooked vacuums in the market, you move in with your own property ploy.

So our next task was to "ride the market," or check out the existing Turner billboards, and see where they were placed, how well they were maintained and where we might conceivably fit in. We also talked discreetly with advertisers in the Atlanta area, and we found that a number of them were dissatisfied with the outdoor advertising service they were getting.

Of course, this sort of dissatisfaction isn't at all uncommon in any sort of real estate business, especially one like the Atlanta situation, which at the time involved a monopoly company with a wide variety of other business interests. We learned that many advertisers were unhappy with the quality of the structures that were available and also with the attitude of some of the Turner employees they had to deal with.

All this was old hat to me. I had heard it all before in other markets, in other parts of the country. I knew people had said the same things about me in some of my real estate ventures. For example, you'll recall how the super-broker, Phil Miller, had checked my motel's reputation in Oak Ridge, Tennessee, and had discovered all sorts of complaints and criticisms. I knew that many of them were true because even though I had put a lot of money and effort into that motel, it wasn't my main real estate venture at the time and also I was having to run it as an absentee owner a couple of hundred miles away.

Turner, likewise, had his sports teams, television interests and other involvements, and so he couldn't devote all his time to his billboard business. The result was that there were weaknesses in the way that it was run. And successful as it was, it was those weaknesses and deficiencies that beckoned to me as overlooked real estate opportunities that could put money in my pocket and the pockets of my investors.

So the circumstances were right for somebody to enter the market and do quite well where Turner was falling short. We knew if we could offer advertisers first-rate structures and a professional group of concerned people to deal with, we'd have a good chance to succeed.

To be able to compete effectively, we did an even closer study of exactly how the Turner organization was operating in the Atlanta market. We concentrated especially on the physical quality of their billboards because we knew that these structures would be the bottom line when we were going to advertisers to argue that we could do a better job. We had to know our competitors as well or better than they knew themselves.

And that's an important principle for you to keep in mind if you're girding yourself to do battle with a company already in business in a given market: Study them so that you know their strengths and weaknesses as well as you know your own.

We looked at everything about those Turner boards: their "impression value" (or their visual impact), their average height, the direction in which they faced, and the quality of their illumination. We also did a close investigation of how well the billboards were maintained: Did the paper have a lot of cracks, loose "flags" or peels? Or did the boards look poor because the company had pasted one too many posters on top of the other, without scraping off the paper underneath?

We also checked how many dollars the advertisers were being charged per billboard, and on this basis we calculated that if we could build at least 300 or so of these structures in the Atlanta market, we could survive quite nicely.

The next problem we faced was what kind of price and terms we should offer our advertisers to be able to compete most effectively with Turner. But to understand how we arrived at our decision, it's necessary first of all to understand something about how advertisers and billboard operators evaluate proper coverage of a market.

The basic reference point for billboard coverage of any market is what's called a "number 100 showing." This term refers to the number of billboards needed to reach 100 percent of the population in a given market in a twenty-four-hour period. At the time we were setting up our business, Atlanta was a market of 1.8 million people. So to have a number 100 showing there, it was necessary first to calculate the traffic flow that passed certain locations around the city during a twenty-four-hour period. Then, the billboard operator would place billboards at certain strategic points so that they reached at least 1.8 million people in the required twenty-four hours.

The Turner company required advertisers to buy 128 billboards for a number 100 showing at that time, but I thought it would be interesting for us, as the "new boy in town," to find locations that could deliver approximately the same circulation with fewer billboards. If we charged the same price per billboard and got the same impact with fewer of them, this would be a real incentive for advertisers to come with us.

We found that the locations we originally leased allowed us to offer a number 100 showing for only 112 billboards, as opposed to the competition's 128. So we decided to build 336 poster panels as soon as we went into the market, which would be enough boards for three number 100 showings.

To increase our income, we decided to offer only a 10 percent discount for advertisers who bought one of our packages for twelve months—in contrast to Turner's discount of 20 percent. But still, our basic prices would be lower since we estimated we could achieve the same impact as the competition with fewer boards. And we resolved to work very hard to provide better maintenance and higher quality service than Turner Advertising.

To enhance the quality of our real estate product still

further, we planned to use mostly single-panel billboards —or one advertisement that faced in any given direction, so that most of our advertisers would not be competing with anyone else. Turner Advertising, in contrast, frequently had multiple facings per location. This is usually an acceptable practice in most markets. But the multiple-facing technique just doesn't have as good an impression value as one billboard all by itself. We thought this single-panel approach would be an ideal showcase for national advertisers interested in a particularly strong showing in the Atlanta market—especially since our rates were competitive.

We were now moving into the home stretch in our preliminary planning. Before we put up a single board, though, we wanted to line up at least one major advertiser who would back us from the start. And we also got busy obtaining new leases for the locations we wanted and converting some of Lawrence Reese's old junior panel leases for our big boards.

But we held off filing any applications for permits with local authorities because we knew the competitor would catch wind of our activities immediately if we did that. As it was, we were fairly sure that some of the property owners we had contacted had turned right around and called Turner Advertising to see if they could get a better deal from them for a lease. Despite our increasing activity, however, the Turner people apparently took little notice. After all, as far as they knew this was another Reese company, and they were thoroughly familiar with his mode of operations, which they presumed would focus on the smaller, non-threatening junior panels.

We did run into a few points of resistance as we moved around trying to pick up leases, but that was to be expected in a highly competitive market. The Turner people had locked up leases for a lot of prime sites in Atlanta for long periods of time and had even filed permits for these locations, even though they hadn't yet bothered to put up any billboards. But their permits meant that no one else could build on those properties.

We did pick up some choice sites in the heart of Atlanta, but we also started looking for locations on the outskirts of the city proper, in Cobb County and Gwinnett County. These two counties were exploding overnight in business and residential growth. Except for the residential areas, we found we could build almost anywhere we wanted in these counties. So here we had found at least one gigantic opportunity.

As a matter of fact, some of our advertisers told us at first, "The Turner people say you can't build in those counties. It's real difficult."

But that just turned out to be incorrect: Apparently the competition didn't feel like spending money on new structures in those areas. Sometimes, when you're the only guy in the market, as Turner Advertising was at that point, you don't have much incentive to go out and aggressively search for new leases. It's easy to get complacent without any strong competition. But we expected their attitude in that regard to change quite soon.

It wasn't long before we had secured enough leases for 250 billboards, and we had done it without waking the "giants" of the business or even causing them to shift uncomfortably in their sound sleep. You might say we were just filling a void or vacuum in the market rather than pushing Turner aside, and that's exactly what I'm getting at when I talk about finding overlooked opportunities in heavy competition.

But we didn't expect them to continue to be unconcerned or complacent when they found out about us. So we continued to move forward quickly and maintained our cloak of secrecy. Finally, we got enough sites to "ride" a representative from a major ad agency around the Atlanta area. We all piled into a car and drove him to the locations where our boards would be placed. After a few such visits, it became obvious to him that we had a serious, quality operation that was about to get off the ground, and he became very enthusiastic, even excited.

Finally, after we had returned to my office, he said he would recommend to his client that they not only buy 112 boards for a number 100 showing, but that they buy them for twelve months out of the year—and probably continue the relationship for the next several years. So he picked sixty or seventy sites that seemed prime locations to him, and we agreed to turn them over to his advertising agency as soon as we put the billboards up. Also, we agreed to concentrate all our initial efforts on the locations he approved and to build our structures by a certain date, so that his company would be the first to advertise in our new market.

Now we had reached the end of our planning, and the time had come to act. We had one big national advertiser, and we also knew of a number of local businesses that were willing to go with us. So D Day had arrived. In this sort of competitive situation, if you can keep your plans secret until the last moment, as we had done, the most effective tactic is to start putting up your billboard structures like a blitzkrieg attack. You don't fool around; you don't delay for any reason. You just put up those boards overnight if possible and go for other advertisers as though your life depended on it. At the same time, however, it's wise to scatter your construction throughout the market so that a proliferation of billboards does not negatively affect the community.

Remember: We're talking about a *highly* competitive situation here, and you can assume that the guy on the other side isn't going to sit still when the magnitude of what you're doing registers with him. The faster you move, the more likely you are to keep him off balance and maintain the offensive. You're very vulnerable during the first stages of your actual "attack" on the market, and your competitor may be in a strong enough position to give you some real setbacks if you don't strengthen and solidify your position as soon as possible.

To be sure that our building operations would go smoothly and also to maintain that state of secrecy right until the last moment, we hired a construction company that I had known from Erie, Pennsylvania. They came in with instructions to build those single-panel billboards we had settled upon. Then, at the last moment, we secured our building permits and immediately began our crash construction program.

We threw those billboards up at a furious rate—more than ten a week. The full 336 structures that we had planned were built in an eight-month period, between September 1978 and April 1979. By the time the Turner people had girded themselves for combat and were making their moves against us in areas like Cobb and Gwinnett Counties, we'd already finished there. We had all the leases we needed in those counties, and we had built all our structures.

By this time the Turner organization was well aware of what we were doing. And their frustrations started to build. I was told by one mutual acquaintance that Turner's billboard people had at one point set up a makeshift war room in their offices, with a huge map of the Atlanta market on the wall and pins to mark our lease sites. I even heard that one of their top executives got so angry at the situation that he told his people to stop putting pins into the map because it was too demoralizing.

We were now truly a force to be reckoned with. And

it had happened, or seemed to have happened, almost overnight. But Reese and I both knew that years of thinking and months of extensive planning had gone into the lightning strike we had staged in the Atlanta billboard market.

Turner was a tough competitor, however, and soon he was giving us the stiffest kind of competition in those areas where our billboards overlapped. Some of our boards were built in Turner's strongest territory, and we found that neither of us could push the other out of the market. Instead, sometimes an advertiser who had come to "ride a showing" (or check the effectiveness) of Turner's boards —or of ours, for that matter—would wind up giving contracts to *both* of us! In other words, the billboard market was so rich in Atlanta that there was easily room for both of us, even in the most hotly contested areas. We even found that many top national advertisers, like General Motors, had a policy that when they advertised in a market with more than one quality billboard company, they would split their business between them.

So we were an immediate success, and as our success continued to mushroom, I knew, even after we had been in the Atlanta market less than a year, that the time had arrived to start thinking about how we were going to expand. And that brings me to one of the most important principles of this chapter: *Almost from the time you begin a real estate venture, you should begin to plan how you're going to sell your property for a profit.*

Now, this principle could be misunderstood to mean that you should focus on get-rich-quick schemes in your rags-to-riches real estate dealings. But I think you know, by this time, that that's not the way I operate. No, I'm referring to the fact that one of the best ways you can make real money in depressed or overlooked real estate is to build up, beautify or otherwise enhance the value of your property so that it can be sold for multiples of what it originally cost.

In the case of our Atlanta billboard venture, I had no intention of making this business my life's work. So from the very start, I was looking for ways to build up the value of our holdings in view of a possible future sale. An absolute rule that I always adhere to in real estate and any other business is: *Never get into an investment before you have a clear idea about how you're going to get out of it.*

One good sign that we might make a lucrative future sale of our billboard venture was that many new advertisers were coming to us and giving us part of their advertising dollars. That meant we had an attractive approach that was resulting in an ongoing stream of orders and an increasing cash flow—factors that would go far in raising the value of our properties.

A second good portent for the future was that just as we completed the last of our 336 billboards after being in operation for eight months, a large national corporation approached me with an informal offer of $3.2 million for the business. Now that represented much, much more than we had put into the business. You'll recall that between the bank loan and notes from investors we had put about $800,000 into the company up front, and so this corporation was offering us about four times our original investment in less than a year of operations.

But I wasn't too impressed. I thought they were too low, and I told them we'd need $3.7 million to sell out at that point. We had a couple of meetings to discuss the matter, but we couldn't come to terms. They finally told me they just couldn't believe that we were turning down a very respectable offer from such a reputable company.

But I said, "Come back in a year's time, and the going price will be five million dollars."

And I wasn't kidding about that. My investors, associates and I knew what the value of the company was, and we weren't going to be sold short. Instead, we decided to keep on building. But we were a little short on cash to do all we wanted to do, and we didn't want to go through a bank again and pay their uncertain and possibly quite high interest rates.

Here again the future sale of the company was a consideration: If we had taken out a loan with high interest rates, a potential buyer might have worried about our profitability since we would have been putting a squeeze on our cash flow through high monthly payments on big loans to banks.

But we still felt it was important to shoot for about 600 billboard structures before we put the company on the block. The reason was that the more structures we built, the more sales we'd have on the books. And the more sales we had, the greater our operating profit was likely to be. Finally, the greater the operating profit, the more valuable the company.

So we came up with a concept where we could bypass conventional financing and still get our billboards. We got in touch with several people who had wanted to buy into the company but had appeared on the scene too late to be included with the initial investors. We then made an arrangement with them whereby they could put up the capital to build the extra few hundred billboard structures we needed and then they would lease them back to us.

Here's the way this arrangement worked: We figured that the billboards would cost about $3,000 each to construct. So we said our company would agree to lease them for 15 percent per year—which came to $450 annually, or $37.50 a month. At the same time, the typical ground lease we were paying to landowners was about $200 a year per panel, and the average rate we were charging advertisers was about $220 a month, or $2,640 a year.

So if all we had to pay for a billboard was $450 a year to the structure owner and $200 to the landowner, for a total of $650 annually, then we could make out just fine— even if the board only sold out four months each year!

On average, we sold our billboards for nine months out of the year, and in some cases, we were getting entire yearlong commitments from national advertisers. With an eye to the future sale of our business, we reserved the right to assign the lease to a new owner.

This leaseback arrangement for the billboard structures was a good deal for the lessors just as it was for us. They received substantial tax credits, depreciation and cash income.

Soon, the lessors we had lined up had made it possible to build 264 billboards; this gave our company a total of 600, the goal we had set for ourselves at the beginning of our venture. Now, we were ready to look seriously for a buyer. And there were plenty coming out of the woodwork.

I even got a couple of very cordial letters from Ted Turner, in which he suggested that maybe we could get together for a talk. My main problem was that I didn't know what we would do if we *did* get together. I couldn't very well say, "Okay, here's my billboard company. You can buy it for such-and-such a price." The problem, you see, was with the good will I had built up among my advertisers. They were buying space from our company because, for whatever reason, we offered something *different* from Turner. So even though Turner was my logical buyer in that market, I felt an obligation to look elsewhere.

The most attractive offer we got came from Metromedia Inc., the huge national television, outdoor advertising and entertainment company. So we entered into serious negotiations with them and finally hammered out a deal.

They agreed to buy our company, which included the 336 company-owned billboards, plus some painted bulletins we had erected. They also had the right to the leases for the other 264 billboards owned by the lessors along with the option to buy them at a future date if they so chose. In the meantime, however, they agreed to assume the leases and pay the rental as had been agreed under our management.

In return for the company, Metromedia agreed to pay us more than $5 million. So in less than three years of operations, we had used about $800,000 in notes, loans and other investments to build a company worth more than six times the money we had invested in it. Out of the money from Metromedia, we had to pay off the various notes and loans to our investors and to the bank, and so we ended up with about $4.4 million to distribute among our shareholders.

So, as you can see from this illustration, there is every reason to look at least twice before you decide to run away from an intensely competitive real estate situation. Tough competition does indeed reflect a market that may in some respects be extremely hard to break into, much less make a respectable profit. But it may also signal the existence of one or more extremely attractive but overlooked property ploys that can put you well on the way to amassing a fortune in the uncertain 1980s.

But now let's turn away from specific *types* of real estate investment and concentrate more on *techniques* that you should know about as you try to transform poor properties into tremendous profit centers. I call these techniques the "tools of the trade" in rags-to-riches real estate ventures.

9

The Tools of the Trade in Rags-to-Riches Real Estate Deals

As WE'VE EXPLORED the ins and outs of finding and exploiting depressed, neglected and overlooked real estate opportunities, two special investment techniques have appeared on several occasions, and now I'd like to discuss them in more detail.

I'm referring to *options* and *leases*—a couple of practical devices that I believe will become increasingly important in successful real estate deals in this decade. It's especially appropriate that we discuss these two concepts in this book because they have often been ignored or overlooked to the detriment of those who have hoped to make a bundle in property ventures of one type or another.

We'll deal with each of these practical "tools" in turn, and then we'll move on to some thoughts about how you can most effectively finance the property ploys that I'm sure are rattling around in your mind by now.

The Option

The option concept has been around a long time and is often used in speculating on the stock market. But in the real estate field it's an extremely useful device that is often overlooked, even by the most astute investors.

Simply stated, an option is a written agreement whereby the investor (the optionee) puts down a relatively small amount of money on a piece of property and is given the right to purchase or lease that property within a certain specified period of time at an agreed-upon price. If he fails to "exercise" his option within that time—in other words, if he doesn't buy or lease the property—then the landowner who sold him the option (the optionor) gets to keep the option money.

An option agreement can work to the benefit of both parties in a couple of ways. First of all, the landowner who is trying to sell or lease his property gets assured of some income from a prospective buyer right off the bat. Also, he knows as long as the option is in effect that he has a "live one" on the line who may well eventually buy his property.

Secondly, the arrangement works to the benefit of the prospective buyer because he doesn't have to put all the money for the property up at once. Instead, if he has a property ploy in mind that hasn't yet been completely worked out, he will be buying some time with the option to "make it happen" before he actually purchases the property.

But there are also a number of disadvantages. As far as the landowner is concerned, when he sells an option on his property, he automatically takes it off the market. Nobody else can buy that property until the option expires. And if real estate values in his area really begin to soar during the period of the option, he's still bound to the price that he agreed to accept from the optionee—a price that may well be lower than surrounding land values that could be on the rise during a booming economy.

The guy who buys the option also runs a risk. If he can't put his property ploy together or for some other reason decides not to buy the tract of land, he loses all his option money. He has gambled some of his hard-earned cash, and he's lost.

How much should an option be sold for? That's an easy question to answer: The landowner should get as much as he can for the option, and the optionee should pay as little as he can get away with! Seriously, though, it's hard to be much more specific. In a low-traffic suburban or rural area, you might be able to get an option on a $100,000 tract of land for $3,000, or 3 percent of the purchase price. This option might run for a reasonably long period of time—say in excess of a year.

But in a place like Miami Beach or San Francisco, you'd probably have trouble getting an option at all on most property. As options become more common in real estate dealings, I expect the size of options to increase substantially in the next few years, say up to around 10 percent to 15 percent of the purchase price.

How long should an option run? Again, that's an easy one to answer in some respects: The landowner should limit the option to as short a period as he possibly can so that he won't tie up his property in the event that land values around him start to go up. Also, he may need to get income from the property, and the option could be an impediment. The one seeking the option, on the other hand, will want the option period to run as long as possible so that he can have plenty of flexibility in setting up his property idea and his financing before he decides whether it's really worth his while to buy.

As a general rule of thumb, I would say that a guy who buys an option for one month is a rank gambler. You really have to be on a fast pair of roller skates to put a deal together of any significance within thirty days—that is, unless you have *already* more or less put it into place and need only thirty days to be sure some small piece in your property puzzle is going to materialize.

An individual who buys an option for a year is a little better off, but I'd say he's not really ultrasmart. A year goes by pretty quickly if you have a lot to do to put your real estate deal together. So if you give yourself only twelve months, you're going to have some high anxieties at various points because you'll be acutely aware that the meter's running when certain things you expect to happen by a certain time don't occur until a month or so later.

Finally, the person who has managed to negotiate an option for two or three years is showing the best business judgment. In three years, particularly, there is a great likelihood that the real estate market will change substantially in different parts of the country. If you can buy that much time with an option payment, you'll find you have time to put your concept together, get your financing nailed down, and perhaps even come out well ahead with the price you've fixed in your option agreement—provided that real estate prices have gone up substantially while you've been holding the option.

But I don't want to give the impression that it's always a smart idea—even if you can negotiate a relatively low option price and a fairly long period during which to exercise it—to go out automatically and throw your money around indiscriminately on pieces of real estate.

Before you even consider an option on a piece of property, ask yourself these questions:

• Do I have a definite prospective customer in the wings who has indicated a willingness to buy the type of property on which I'm about to buy an option?

• Or secondly, do I have a definite property ploy in mind—one that I've talked over with possible investors and tested in some way through market research?

If your answer to these questions is no, I'd say hold off on buying that option. You should be pretty far along in your thinking and planning before you ever put any money down on a deal. But if after thinking about it, you feel the time has arrived to think in terms of an option, here are a few more points to consider.

Most real estate brokers you'll probably deal with won't have much experience with options. And most likely, nearly all of them will resist the idea of having you put an option down on a piece of property rather than buying it outright. Why? Their commission will be less on the option because there's a smaller amount of money involved.

But there are plenty of ways to get a broker interested in an option. First of all, whether you're dealing with a broker or with the landowner himself, you should stress at first that you want to *buy* a certain type of land. The option is just the first step to that end.

Also, when you find the land you want and begin to talk in terms of options, you should immediately pull out your checkbook and prepare to write out a check for whatever amount you can agree upon. That way, with your cash in hand, you show him you mean business. You're not just a talker.

But you don't just hand him the check when you've arrived at an understanding. You first sign an option agreement, stating the amount of money you'll buy the property for if you exercise the option and also the length of the option period. Also, you should put the check in escrow, probably with a local attorney, until the option agreement has been definitely nailed down with the land-owner.

And if it's the broker who is your main contact, you might want to let him in on a little bit of your thinking about what you plan to do with the property. You certainly don't want to bring him completely in on your idea—at least not at first, not until you get to know him a little better. But you can show him that, far from being some scatterbrained out-of-towner, you're a thoughtful, knowledgeable entrepreneur with some financial backing. Then, with a little prompting from you, perhaps he'll begin to realize that if he hooks up with you he might become the broker for other deals you have planned in his area of operations.

When you're negotiating with the broker for the property he'll name the top figure that the seller is asking, even though neither of them expects to get that much. They expect you to make a counteroffer, and the final figure you'll reach will be somewhere in between. But if you have an option deal at the back of your mind you might make it more palatable to the broker—and to the landowner—by trying an approach like this:

Let's say the landowner is asking $100,000 for the property, but then the broker says, "I think you might get it for ninety thousand dollars." Then you respond, "I don't know about that, but what about say eighty thousand dollars?"

"No," the broker might say. "He won't go that low, but we could try something like, say, eighty-seven thousand dollars."

And that's when you hit him with your option: You say, "I'll go you one better. I'll buy it at the full one hundred thousand dollars he's asking—but I want to buy it three years from now. And I'm willing to put some blood on the line right now, some money in his pocket, if he'll go for this."

After the broker recovers, you can start talking about the amount you're willing to pay for a three-year option.

If you begin to deal in options, it's important to realize that all the terms are negotiable. I'd suggest that you get a good real estate attorney to draft up a basic option contract for you to use and to change it as your deals change, from transaction to transaction.

For example, you might want to be sure that any option you pay would be applied against the purchase price of the property. Also, to preserve your rights in the property after you've bought an option on it, it's necessary to file the option at the local land office. An attorney is an important asset to help you ensure you're taking the proper steps.

Also, during the entire negotiations, it's probably a good idea to avoid the use of the word *option* if that's at all possible, because most of the people you're dealing with won't understand the full import of what the term means. The broker *may* understand, but then again he may only have a vague idea of how options can be used. The main thing he's worried about is how much money he can get from the deal he's putting together. And if you can convince him that there's a 90 percent chance you're really going to buy the property, he may support your option idea when he brings the offer to the landowner.

The landowner, for his part, may be convinced when he hears (1) he's ultimately going to get a higher price than he was expecting for the property, even if it is a couple of years in the future, and (2) he's going to get that option money right now, because it will come in very handy for the vacation he plans to take, or whatever.

Now, as I've indicated elsewhere in this book, I've

frequently taken out options on pieces of property before I actually bought it, and many of those deals have turned into quite successful rags-to-riches real estate ventures. But there's one situation I encountered in the wilds of Montana that fell through because of a failure to use an option. Let's take a closer look at that transaction and see what we can learn from the mistakes that were made.

The scene was the Madison River in southeastern Montana in the late 1960s, where five business friends and I were doing some fishing together. We were floating down this beautiful, peaceful river, having a lot of fun with our trout fishing, when I began to notice lots and lots of vacant ground.

Just for conversation's sake, I asked the cowboys who were guiding us on the trip, "How much does this ground cost?"

They said, "Well, you can buy ranches out here—around a thousand or more acres—for about thirty-five to fifty dollars an acre."

One cowboy then pointed to a tract of land over to our right and said, "That one over there is almost exactly one thousand acres, and it's going for three hundred fifty thousand dollars. I know, because it was just put up for sale."

"That's thirty-five dollars an acre," I said.

"Yep, that's what I said."

Some of the properties we floated past had about a mile of river frontage. Later that night a friend of mine, who had been listening to the conversation, said, "Hey, how about us going in together and buying some of this property out here? All I want is the frontage on the river, and you can have the rest of the ground."

His idea was to take this river frontage, break it up into five- or ten-acre lots and sell it off. As for me, I was more interested in the land away from the river because if I owned it I thought I'd probably sell it or lease it out for raising cattle. My wife Ellie's people are grain farmers in Illinois, and I thought it would be a good idea to breed cattle out here in Montana and then bring them back to Illinois to fatten them up so that they could be transported in the best shape possible to the Chicago stockyards.

So I told my friend I was interested in his idea if he could find a piece of property that would suit both of us. A day or so later, I checked with him again because I knew he had been looking around for a tract. "Well, did you find anything?" I asked.

"Yeah," he said. "There was this one piece of property and the guy wanted three hundred thousand dollars for it. It seemed like a pretty good buy."

"Why don't you buy it then?" I asked.

"It's still too expensive."

"What do you mean by 'expensive'?"

"Well," he said, "I just think I could buy it for two hundred fifty thousand dollars."

"Wait a minute," I told him. "Why don't you just give him ten thousand dollars for an option to buy the thing for three hundred thousand dollars. Tie the land up for a couple of years with the option. And then put some ads in *Field and Stream* magazine and *The Wall Street Journal* to see if you can sell the property before you put the entire amount of money down."

Then, I explained my idea in more detail: "If you bought it for even the lower $250,000 figure at $50,000 down, you would pay at least $20,000 monthly at 10 percent interest on the balance. So why not get an option for $10,000? It's less money, and you don't have the downstroke [down payment] of $50,000 tied up."

That seemed like a pretty good idea to him, and so he went back to the real estate broker he had been dealing with. But unfortunately he didn't act quickly enough because the property was sold before he was able to make a deal. He came back to me rather depressed, and I asked him if the buyer would have taken an option if he had moved faster. "Oh, yeah, he would have done it," my friend said. The real estate broker had confirmed that such a proposal would have been accepted.

I could immediately see what had happened here. This man had been too eager to drive a tough bargain with the rancher by using an East Coast, hard-nosed negotiating approach. The problem is that when you're dealing with farmers or others who have been on their property for generations, there is a question of pride involved in any sale of their property. If you try to drive the price down too far, they may interpret your bargaining style as a personal attack on them and on the personal worth of their family's heritage.

One of the best ways I've found to get around this difficulty is the option. Because you're probably tying up the person's property for years into the future with an option arrangement, you can afford to be more lenient on the sales price. And the fact that you're able to give the landowner more for his land means that he's able to keep his pride intact.

So there are many twists and turns to option agreements, and I think you'll find, if you start dealing seriously with neglected or overlooked real estate opportunities, that an option to buy can be a great boon in your efforts. But an equally important tool of the trade that you should consider during the changing real estate climate of the 1980s is the lease.

The Lease

Almost everybody with any basic business sense knows something about a lease. If you have ever lived in an apartment or rented a house, you most likely had to sign a lease, or an agreement to pay a landlord a certain amount of money each month in return for the right to live on the premises.

But leases have many more uses than those that are part of our common experience with urban and suburban housing. As a matter of fact, I can envision the day when many of the most lucrative real estate deals will be done on the basis of leasing rather than buying property. And I believe that the more you know about the concept of the lease, the more adept you'll be at making a profit in any phase of the real estate business.

As I see it, one of the problems with trying to buy real estate in the future is that good quality commercial land is likely to be quite expensive. And if interest rates stay generally high, it will be hard to find acceptable mortgage financing for prospective property owners without seriously cutting into their cash flow. A monthly payment for a lease on the land only, on the other hand, is likely to be much less expensive than an outright purchase or mortgage financing.

You see, most businessmen and many real estate entrepreneurs are primarily interested in the *buildings* that are on the land rather than the land itself, because it's the buildings that generate the cash flow. That was one of the things that Larry Cahill and his company, which bought my Holiday Inn in Oak Ridge, Tennessee, had in mind. I gave them a lease on the land for forty-nine years and as a result was able to offer the property at a lower price than if I had been required to sell the land outright. At the same time, I kept the land in my estate, so that my heirs will get it when the lease expires, and I insured myself and my family of a steady stream of rental income over the next few decades.

As for the buyers, they didn't care at all about the land: The main thing that they were interested in was what they could do during the foreseeable future with the buildings on the land—the motel and its related structures. And a forty-nine-year lease was more than enough time for them to do whatever they liked with that motel property.

This pattern of real estate transaction reflects what I expect will become the norm in this country during the next few decades—just as it has in many parts of Europe. Why? The main reason is that top-value land is getting more and more scarce. There is just so much beachfront property, just so much prime real estate in our great urban centers, and so on. So leases are likely to become a dominant wave of the future in property transactions.

If you happen to be the landowner who is considering a lease, there are a number of things you should keep in mind before you sign an agreement with a prospective lessee. In my opinion the most important element from the landlord's point of view in almost any lease—especially in those leases that run for long terms, such as five years or longer—is the existence of adequate *escalation clauses* in the rents provided for by the lease. These clauses protect the landowner against the erosive action of inflation in our economy because they establish a means for the rents to be raised periodically according to certain reasonable and mutually acceptable guidelines.

For example, you've already seen in my Holiday Inn sale that I obtained a flat yearly rental for a ten-year period for the land on which the motel was built. Then I asked for and received the right after ten years to get a rent based on a percentage of the motel's room sales, if that figure was higher than the original annual figure.

Another way to build in an escalation arrangement is to attach your rents to rises in the consumer price index—the method used by many big-city landlords who rent space in office buildings to various businesses.

Personally, I prefer the percentage-of-sales approach whenever you can get it—provided that you have confidence in the earning power *and* the staying power of the business to which you're leasing your property. I had that kind of confidence in Larry Cahill and his team, and, as a matter of fact, I've learned just as I'm finishing up this book that the Holiday Inn I sold to him only a few months ago in Oak Ridge has become his second most profitable motel among the twenty that he operates.

Of course, each real estate deal you set up will be a little different from the last. But the main principle here is that, whenever possible, you should peg your lease payments to some percentage of the income stream that your lessee will be getting from the business he's conducting on your property.

From the vantage point of the lessee, on the other hand, things look a little different. In the first place, he'd usually rather not commit any of his future earnings to the landowner through a percentage of his business's income stream. But sometimes, the prospect of paying out a percentage is much more attractive than having to fork out a huge amount of money in a down payment and in large monthly mortgage payments that are weighed down by onerous interest rates.

That's the situation I've frequently faced in my own billboard businesses. I'd almost always rather lease than buy, primarily because I prefer to keep my monthly costs as low as possible and, as a result, my cash flow high. The higher the cash flow, the more flexibility I have to make further investments in my property and, hence, to increase my income.

Of course, sometimes you can combine a lease and a purchase with attractive benefits to both parties. Let me illustrate through an experience I had in Terre Haute, Indiana. I bought a small piece of property up there for about $1,200 and erected four billboards on it. But then a funeral home owner came to me and said, "You own that property, don't you? I'd like to buy it and build a floral shop on it."

That sounded good to me, but when he offered me $7,500, I turned him down because I thought the land had gone up in value more than that since I had purchased it. In my opinion it was worth about $15,000, and I wasn't inclined to go any lower. Also, I figured that I'd make more just by holding the property and taking in the income I was getting from the billboards.

But the man still wanted it, and so we got together with my accountant, who suggested, "Bill, why don't you just lease him the ground for ten years at one thousand dollars a year? He can go ahead and build his floral shop on it. And then he can write off the construction costs of the shop over ten years as a leasehold improvement. Finally, at the end of ten years, he could have an option to buy the ground for ten thousand dollars."

Now the proposal was starting to sound more interesting to me—as it was to the funeral home owner. He would get all sorts of high tax write-offs that he wouldn't qualify for if he owned the ground. At the same time, I would get an increased income stream and also a nice lump sum at the end of the lease to finish off the deal. And we even managed to arrange to keep two of the billboards on the property under a forty-year-lease agreement with him! In other words, the lessor-lessee relationship flip-flopped 180 degrees by the time we had reached our final agreement.

It seems clear to me that creative lease deals of this type are sure to be the wave of the future, and that's one very important reason to learn as much about the various uses of a lease as you can. But there's another, less pleasant reason for getting to know the lease tool as intimately as you can: You see, there are all sorts of ways of undercutting or playing tricks on competitors with leases.

In the billboard business, for example, you can get cut right out of a market through practices like "lease-jumping," which is a danger I'd like to illustrate for you through a property deal that I worked on recently in one particularly attractive market in the Southeast.

I set up a billboard company in one of the prime markets in a big beach resort area and, as was my practice, I pulled together several investors including myself—there were seven of us all together—who put up a total of $150,000. This was divided into $130,000 in notes and another $20,000 in stock. Then, we went to a local bank and borrowed $250,000 more, to give us a total of $400,000 for our venture.

As I've already said, I always try to least most if not all of the properties on which I place billboards because it's cheaper than owning the actual land. So I hired three or four employees whose jobs involved nothing but scouring the territory to find suitable property for leases for our billboards.

Within a few months, we had a sufficient number of leases to build about 160 billboard faces in that market. We also got to work lining up some advertisers, and soon we landed one juicy national contract even before the first billboard was built. Since 160 had been our ultimate target, we knew the time for planning had ended and the time for action had arrived. So we went to a local government office to get our permits and were expecting to get off the starting blocks immediately with our construction and, as I had done in Atlanta, erect those billboards as quickly as we could.

But this situation wasn't quite like Atlanta. We had been trying to operate as secretly as possible, but the competition found out about us, and the competition was as intense as any I've ever experienced.

The first big roadblock was thrown up in our path right there in the local property offices. Someone told the county commissioners that he knew for a fact that we were going to do certain things with our billboards that we had no intention of doing. We denied the allegations, but the desired impact had been made by our opponents, and the commissioners passed an emergency ordinance that prevented us from building sixty of the major billboard structures we wanted to erect.

We brought in our lawyers and fought the charges, and finally we were given the right to put up our boards. But there were greater restrictions than we had originally been planning on. For example, we were prevented from building our signs within 500 feet of any other billboard structures that had already been put up.

Also, we were forced to delay the construction of our sites for at least a couple of months, and so all the advantages of speed and surprise had been lost. Our competitors were then able to gird themselves for our foray into their market and tighten up their act with their advertisers.

We also had some indications that certain of our opponents were engaging in what is called "lease-jumping" in the trade. That means that a competitor's lease person would go around to the property owners we had contacted and try to get them to switch from leases with us to leases with the competition.

This problem demonstrates one of the fundamental

weaknesses of having a lease rather than the complete ownership of the property: Even though a lease gives you a definite interest in the property which can be relied upon and defended in court, your interest is nevertheless regarded by many people as less substantial than that of the actual landowner. In other words, it's often much harder to throw the landowner off his property than it is the leaseholder, who may get some damages for any injury to his rights or property interests but who will still often be placed in an inferior position to that of the actual owner.

Now, in any area of real estate, lease-jumping is a real no-no. But still it's done in intensely competitive markets all over the country, and it's something *you* should watch for as well, no matter what field of real estate you choose. You can always take the offenders to the courts, both federal and local, for this sort of thing. And sometimes, despite how expensive and time-consuming court fights can be, you have to take formal legal steps to protect your interests. In our case it might have come to that result had not something quite extraordinary happened to change our whole business situation.

We had heard that there was a hurricane brewing down in the Caribbean, and we decided that since we had been hit with delays because of the legal proceedings and had lost the advantage of surprise, we might as well wait until it blew over. We were planning to ship down steel kits and frames to build our billboards, and we were afraid they might get damaged if the hurricane blew through this area. I might also add that those of us who believed in prayer were seeking divine guidance a great deal during this period because of all the troubles we were facing.

As it happened, the decision to hold off on the construction of the billboards at that time was the most important one that we made in this entire real estate venture. When the hurricane did hit, it almost completely demolished the other billboard structures in the area. We, of course, had no losses at all because we hadn't moved into the area yet.

So we waited for some of the wreckage to be cleared away and then moved immediately to build our structures. But then, when some of our opponents started to rebuild *their* billboards, they found they were prevented from doing so by the very ordinances that some of them had fought so hard to get passed against us. For example, there was that ordinance that said you couldn't erect one billboard within 500 feet of another, but now *ours* were the ones that were in place rather than theirs! We had brand-new permits, and the competition could not rebuild in those newly restricted arteries.

So finally, even though we had the upper hand in this situation, I was ready to negotiate anytime a good offer might come along. And one wasn't too long in coming, either. Another big billboard outfit near where we had been staging this pitched battle over leases approached us with a serious proposal.

We finally settled on a price of $850,000 cash for the 160 billboards we had built. That meant that after we paid off all our loans to the bank and to our stockholders, we had a capital gain of $450,000 after only about one year of operations. My share of that was 75 percent of the stock, or about $337,500.

Now throughout this discussion and some of the others in this book, you may have been a little disconcerted by the fact that I *always* have a majority interest in these companies, and sometimes it's a rather large majority interest. But let me explain something in case you haven't picked it up already: The person who is the active investor —the one who is putting the deal together and really making it happen—is almost always the one who has the biggest interest in any venture.

And that's always the role I play. In most cases, the other investors are passive participants who put up money for notes and stock but who don't participate directly in the strategy planning and operations of any of these real estate ventures. In contrast, I'm the one who puts in the most time and has the background in these transactions to guide them from start to finish. And it's a common practice in the industry that a leading role in this sort of real estate "play" should always be rewarded with a larger percentage of the equity of the company.

In addition, usually I am the only one who signs a personal note with the bank that is providing the financial backing for the venture. This added risk that I assume is another factor to consider in granting additional ownership privileges in a company.

The reason I mention these points is not just to let you know that I'm not being greedy about the percentage I take. Rather, the key point is that you should evaluate your own interests and talents and consider whether you're best suited to be a passive or active investor in any real estate venture. In some business deals, I put up my money and remain in the background. But when it comes to most real estate ventures that fall into the rags-to-riches category—the depressed, neglected or overlooked property opportunities—I usually try to get into the driver's seat. Why? Both because I like the excitement and also because I often have the experience to have a good shot at success.

So these, then, are a few words and illustrations to give you an overview of the two key tools of the trade that are becoming increasingly essential aids for those who want to transform seemingly poor property into good profits.

But this book wouldn't be complete without some final observations on what it takes to achieve successful financing for a rags-to-riches real estate venture. So now let's spend a little time pondering some ways to magnify the money you have—no matter how little it may be—so that it can do more things for you than you ever thought possible.

10

How to Finance Your
Property Deal
with Mirrors
Instead of Money

ONE LAWYER FRIEND of mine from Indiana accompanied me to a million-dollar real estate deal I was trying to put together in Washington, D.C., and one of the keys to that deal was arranging the financing. We met all the principals, including the broker, in a big law firm in Washington, and we negotiated all the way to the point at which we were ready to close.

I had agreed to put about $40,000 in this million-dollar cash deal but I owned 60 percent of the equity in our newly formed company which was to acquire the assets of the seller. The broker, who was an acquaintance of mine from way back, stood to make a 6 percent commission on the million, or about $60,000.

He was a good broker, but he had done something to me that I regarded as a sort of practical joke that hurt just a little too much, and I was eager to put one over on him as well. You see, he had told me that he would leave his commission in as an investment in a piece of property that I had bought back in the Midwest. But when we got down to the wire and were ready to close the deal, he told me he had arranged for me to get a loan from a local bank

201

instead. In other words, I'd have to pay off that loan if I wanted to go through with the deal rather than have his interest-free investment in the form of his commission.

Now, in this Washington negotiation, I thought I saw an opportunity to have some fun myself. So just as we were about to put all our money and signed contracts in the ring and close, I called for a recess. I then grabbed the broker by the hand and walked him out into the hall.

"You know," I said, "I really can't go through with this deal today because I don't have the money to pay for my end of it."

He almost dropped dead in his tracks. "What do you mean?"

"I mean I don't have the forty thousand dollars I need to close."

"But the deal will fall through!"

"I know," I said. "But you can help me. All I need is forty thousand dollars of your sixty-thousand-dollar commission."

He had to agree, otherwise he wouldn't get a cent out of this sale. So I walked back into the room with 60 percent of the equity cost—and not a dime of my own money on the line.

As we were on our way home, my lawyer friend who had accompanied me to the closing said, "You know, Dooñer, you don't use money. You do your deals with mirrors!"

By that he meant that I always *seemed* to have money that I was investing here and there, but actually most of the riches I was flashing around came from other people and other sources like banks, not my own pocket.

Now there is some truth in my friend's observation: I do try to finance my deals with "mirrors" in that I don't rely primarily on my own money to increase my investment holdings. In a sense, I suppose you could say that I "reflect" other people's cash in that an important part of my investment skills involve pulling together money from many different investors and a variety of banks. And then I begin to make it work for me, and them, by applying the real estate skills I've developed over the years.

Frequently, I don't even need "outside" money, for my track record with banks is excellent. But I use outside-investor financing for personal motivation. I'm much more cautious with other people's money (or "OPM" as we call it), and I like the challenge to make good capital gains for other individuals.

But it's not really fair to say that I operate *only* with "mirrors" because that could imply that there is little substance to the transactions I put together. And it could also imply that I don't put any of my own "blood," or cash, into my ventures—but as you've seen, that's just not the case. Except in very rare instances, I *always* put a substantial amount of my own money into my property deals. And, perhaps most important of all, I am almost always the only investor who signs a personal note to guarantee the big loans that we secure from banks, which finance a large part of most of our operations.

But even though I'm opposed to the wheeler-dealer, trickster-like approach that is often associated with the "mirrors" type of financing that my friend was jokingly referring to, there is an important principle involved here: And that is that *it's important to use every financial and tax device that is legally available to free as many dollars as possible in order to maintain a high cash flow.*

A healthy cash flow is the life blood of every successful business. If you can keep the cash coming in so that you not only pay off your overhead and expenses but also have enough to keep building your business up more and making additional investments, you almost *have* to succeed. But if your cash flow drops precariously low, even dipping below what you need to break even on your expenses, you're in deep trouble—and may well be on your way to failure.

Most businesses these days fail simply because they run out of enough money to keep their operations going. Some people say these businesses are undercapitalized—a term that just means they didn't have enough money at the beginning to cover their costs until they had been operating long enough to get a solid cash flow going. And that gets back to the idea that I try to finance with "mirrors." I suppose I do hold up a lot of mirrors when I go around trying to get people to invest in my ventures.

But those mirrors don't reflect fantasies. The images in them are real investors and real banks with real money. My job is just to paint a realistic—and exciting—picture of what that money can eventually turn into, how it can be magnified and reflected in many other ways, if we can just get enough of it to accomplish a given real estate goal. In other words, I try to do all I can to get plenty of passive investment money into the business at the very beginning so that there is little chance that I'll run into a cash-flow problem.

But before we go any further, let's define our terms more precisely: What exactly *is* cash flow? Cash flow is essentially the same thing as operating profit, and it's defined a little differently from business to business in the real estate field. In the hotel or motel business, for example—which is typical of many other businesses—cash flow is the operating profit that a business earns after all direct overhead and expenses are taken out but *before* payment of taxes and debt service, such as interest expenses and depreciation.

In other words, if you had $1,000 in sales at a motel, you might have a 30 percent operating profit, or $300, after subtracting all overhead costs and expenses. That

$300 would be your cash flow. Then, from your cash flow, you would still have to subtract all your taxes, except income tax, and also all payments to debt service, including interest and principal payments you're making on any loans. The amount you have left after these last subtractions would be available for you to reinvest or to distribute among your shareholders.

In the billboard business, on the other hand, cash flow is defined as the operating profit before payment of taxes. In other words, all you have to subtract from your cash flow is your debt service, and then the balance is free and clear, ready to use as you and your fellow investors like.

The problem in many businesses, however, is that their cash flow starts to shrink or disappear and they find they can't meet those big debt obligations they have to the bank. The biggest safety factor that a fledgling real estate venture has is a healthy cash flow so that there is no threat of a bank foreclosure on the property. So many of your financing efforts in the early days of your business must be directed toward keeping that cash flow as large as possible.

To achieve this end there are a number of principles I've discovered over the years that I'd now like to share with you. Some of them, perhaps many of them, you've already heard about. But I'm going to assume that you know next to nothing about the principles of financing a real estate venture at this point because I certainly didn't know a thing when I started out.

As a matter of fact, when one of my first mentors, the billboard magnate Robert Naegele, once asked me if I had a cash-flow projection for one of my small businesses, I thought he had come in off the moon. I had no idea what he was talking about.

I had to learn everything about real estate financing while I was *doing* it, and a lot of that learning was by trial and error. But I was also quite lucky to have two key people who sort of served as an informal faculty for my on-the-job "business school."

One, as I said, was Bob Naegele, whom I described in an earlier chapter as the most creative and innovative person in the billboard business when I was just starting out. He was the man who revamped the old billboard structures and gave them much better illumination and appearance. But what he taught me about financing was just as important as what he taught me about selling. In short, he taught me how to *make* money and how to increase my cash flows and operating profits by streamlining my operations.

Another important man in my early development as a fledgling real estate financier was a fellow named George Shields. A friend who was a spiritual as well as a financial adviser to me before he died, he taught me how to *use* money, especially how to borrow it in the wisest ways. Don't analyze it, utilize it—that is a principle of money management that I can trace back to Shields. And ever since my conversations with him, I've tried never to sit on my funds or those supplied by other people, but to keep working and thinking of ways to get that money to make more money.

Now here are some basic principles of real estate finance that I picked up from these two men, from my trial-and-error "courses" in various parts of the country and from a variety of other sources. They're not listed in any particular order of importance because I've found *each* of them to be crucial at one time or another in my career.

• *Depreciation is a key to cash flow.* This was a concept that I simply couldn't understand when it was first explained to me. I understood that cars and trucks and other things with working parts could depreciate and eventual-

ly fall apart after you'd used them for a while. But some-
how the idea of applying this concept to buildings and
structures on a piece of land didn't sink in at first.

But then, as Bob Naegele showed me how billboards
could become weathered and develop dents and corro-
sion, and how the same sort of thing could happen to
seemingly indestructible buildings, I began to get the picture.

And I also became aware of how important this concept is to cash flow because anytime you can depreciate
a physical asset over a number of years, you can write the
monetary equivalent of that depreciation off on your income tax as a business deduction. This means that you
reduce the taxes you owe, and thus you increase your
operating profit or cash flow. And so I quickly discovered
that depreciation of billboards and other structures could
serve as a shelter from income tax for much if not all of
the money I made from those assets.

I once said, only half-facetiously, that I would fire any
manager who made a profit for me. And by that I meant
that I expect those in our management to be as astute
about the tax consequences of our real estate investments
as they are about actually increasing our income. I said it
once, and I still feel that way!

• *Go for multiple investment tax credits.* Here, again
was a concept that I thought had come in straight off the
moon when I first heard about it. But it's a great compan-
ion to depreciation in providing a comfortable shelter
from income taxes.

The idea of this concept, in case you don't already
know, is that when you invest your money in certain business property you're allowed to take a certain percentage
of your investment right off the income tax you owe as a
credit. It's even better than a deduction against gross

income because you figure the tax first and then subtract your percentage.

For example, I learned if you bought a billboard for $3,000, you could take 10 percent of that figure, or $300, right off your taxes. So if you owed $25,000 in taxes, you would subtract the "ITC" and end up owing only $24,700, and perhaps even less if the depreciation has not been charged against income before you arrive at the $25,000 tax liability.

And then my imagination began to run wild. You see, I suddenly realized that if you owned sixty of those bill-boards and your basic tax bill was $25,000, you could reduce your tax to less than $10,000! I could see all sorts of possibilities for using this information as a sales device in talking with potential investors. And I could also see many advantages for me personally as I prepared to file my own income tax returns.

● *Learn as much about financing as you can from your bank.* You'd be surprised at the number of people who look upon their banker as an adversary rather than a friend. It's true that you may often be in the position of trying to get the bank to lend you some money. But in the long run, they want to help you earn money because that means they'll earn more money as well.

● *Accrual bookkeeping can be the Achilles' heel of a small real estate operation.* It's easy, if you're just invest-ing in property as a sideline business, to be sloppy in your record keeping. But I'd urge you to clean up your act as quickly as possible. Not only will you most likely miss some important tax breaks if you fail to keep good books, but you'll also be quite likely to run into serious cash-flow problems because you may fail to anticipate unusual ex-penses.

For example, I had to learn the hard way from my friend and attorney-accountant, Richard Hammel, that I had to set aside money I had to pay once a year for insurance policies on my properties. More than once, I forgot that a lump-sum payment was due on a certain date, and the result was that I experienced a dip in my cash as I scrambled to pay off the bill.

• *Every successful business must be in debt.* The only way you can hope to turn a piece of poor or depressed property into a fortune is to use *leverage.* And that means you have to borrow, borrow, borrow—as much money as you possibly can to get your real estate venture off the ground and onto the boards as a money-maker. I once said, "If my business doesn't have any debt, I'm either complacent or a slob." And I must say, I still feel that way!

• *Every successful real estate entrepreneur limits the percentage of his debt service in relation to his cash flow.* I firmly believe that you have to borrow money to make money. But at the same time it's important to keep an eye on how much of your cash flow you're using to service your debt. I don't think it's possible to lay down any hard-and-fast guidelines here because each business is a little different from the next.

But generally speaking if the percentage of your debt service begins to creep up to 40 percent or 50 percent of your cash flow, you should become watchful because you could be heading onto dangerous ground. As we've seen before, the death knell of many businesses occurs when their cash flow disappears into their debt service, and they find they can't pay off their bank loans.

• *Be prepared to give a personal guarantee on bank loans if you want to be the controlling investor in any real estate deal.* I know many financial advisers caution against becoming personally liable on business loans. But as a practical matter you won't be able to borrow the money you need to turn a poor piece of property into a rich one unless someone signs the bank loans personally.

Of course, it's quite possible—in fact, quite common and highly advisable—not to sign a bank loan personally if you're one of the minority stockholders in a real estate venture. But if you want to put the deal together and become entitled to a majority interest in the equity, you have to put more "blood" into it than anyone else. And that means not necessarily more up-front money but rather your name and all your personal assets on the dotted line that the bank puts in front of you.

I don't know how many times I've seen a guy go in to borrow $300,000 or so from a bank, and he's got about $50,000 of seed money to show them he's serious. But then they want him to give them a personal guarantee, along with his wife's signature, and he replies, "I won't give it!"

The bankers, in every case I've known about, just respond, "Well, if this deal isn't reliable enough for you to put yourself on the line, it's certainly not good enough for us!"

A personal guarantee shows some courage and confidence in the venture you're proposing, and it reflects the kind of nerve and personality it takes to make a difficult real estate deal happen. So I would go so far as to say that it's best to stay on the back seat as an investor if you're not willing to risk your personal assets.

These financial principles barely scratch the surface of all that you'll need to know to make a successful foray into the field of depressed or overlooked real estate. But they represent a few of the most important highlights of the things I've learned, often the hard way, in trying to make big money from some of my property ploys.

At this point it would be easy just to sign off and free you to try your hand at your own property ploy in rags-to-riches real estate. After all, we've covered most of the key principles that, when mastered, can enable you to make a go of it. But there are still a couple of things I'd like to say to you before we part company—some things that you may find rather helpful as you embark on your search for a fortune in today's uncertain economy.

11

...to Riches

WE'VE COVERED a great deal of ground in the preceding pages, and much of what we've been discussing has been very detailed and specific. But now I'd like to ask you to step back for a moment from the nitty-gritty of neglected real estate and take a look at the big picture of where we've been and especially where *you're* going.

First of all, the main purpose of this book has not been to provide you with a step-by-step, mechanical blueprint of how to take a piece of property and turn it into a million dollars. I can't do that for you, and neither can any other person or book.

But what I hope to have done is to stimulate you to think more expansively and creatively about how to apply your own special interests and skills in the real estate market. There are many properties out there that are lying unused or poorly used. And with a little money and effort, you could be in an excellent position to begin to turn them into something useful, productive and highly profitable.

The key element in succeeding in this field is to find a way to fit that part of your personality that is most enthusiastic and easy to motivate to the right piece of property. Land, as I've said many times in these pages, is not a static item that you buy and sit on. It's a *dynamic* thing, more a concept than a physical reality.

Land is what you make of it. And the way you make something of a piece of land, a building or any other structure that is an integral part of what we call real estate is to mold it and shape it through ideas.

The vacant land next to filling stations in the Midwest is a useless, unsightly lot to most passing motorists. To me it was a Hen House restaurant chain that is now worth millions of dollars. To you it may well be something quite different but equally valuable.

The point I'm making here is that land and the structures that rise from it have no fixed identity. They are what you *think* they are—and what you, by force of will and hard work, make them.

In a way it all comes down to who you think *you* are. If you believe in yourself and you have the self-confidence to take your innate talents and special skills and apply them in the real estate field, then almost any piece of land might become a major profit center for you.

In this regard you'll recall that I mentioned at the beginning of this book something about developing a property personality, a set of personal traits that can enable you to transform poor real estate into a considerable personal fortune. We've mentioned many different principles and personality characteristics throughout the preceding pages. But let me reiterate just a few that I feel are essential to the property personality.

• *An ability to generate creative ideas that can become the key to turning depressed or little-known property opportunities into a fortune.* These are the so-called property ploys, or business ideas, that we have been talking about throughout this book. The ideas must come first, and then the choice of property, financing and other elements in a successful deal will follow naturally.

• *An adeptness in dealing with competition.* Even if there is no competition at first—which there often will not be in a neglected or overlooked property situation—when you begin to transform your chosen white elephant, you'll find that your competitors start coming out of the woodwork. But there's no reason to be afraid! As we've seen, even if the competition is hot to begin with, there are always plenty of places for an enterprising entrepreneur to make big bucks.

• *A willingness to take a second look at every piece of ugly or unattractive property.* The first look should always give you a negative impression—if it didn't, every other would-be investor would be scrambling after the property! So it's important to condition yourself always to turn back and re-examine that piece of land that you may have initially rejected. Then you'll begin to see possibilities of profit that you missed the first time around.

• *A preference for depressed, neglected or overlooked property opportunities.* If you're automatically drawn to the most beautiful pieces of land that you see, you'll be all too likely to move with the hordes of other people who *overlook* overlooked property.

• *A patience to hold combined with a willingness to sell.* You may make a lot of money very quickly in the "rags" real estate market, but the best deals you'll find won't be the classic get-rich-quick schemes. By this I mean that even though you may be able to come up with a business idea, buy the property, build it up and sell it for a huge profit in a short period of time—sometimes less than a year—it won't be easy. This kind of investment, if you are to be the primary mover in making it happen, requires a great deal of thought and also a considerable amount of hard work.

● *Grim determination.* This trait provides the foundation for all the others. I've used this term elsewhere synonymously with what I think of as a person's fundamental character. Most people I know fall by the wayside in their great career ambitions because they lack a kind of perseverance that must come from deep within, a perseverance that more often than not is rooted in convictions that have nothing directly to do with real estate or business.

In my own case, as you already know, this grim determination appeared only after I overcame my alcohol problem and, eventually, made a commitment to Jesus Christ. In saying this I'm certainly not suggesting that a faith in Christ is a prerequisite to successful real estate investment—far from it! But in my own case the emotional equilibrium and inner drive and ability to persevere in tough business dealings must be attributed in large part to my faith orientation. I know I was incapable of performing with any reasonable success before God got involved. At the same time there are plenty of other successful real estate investors who don't believe the same way I do. However you go about it, it's essential in some way to develop that special kind of drive and commitment that will, among other things, enable you to transform poor property into valuable real estate.

Even as I make these suggestions about how you can develop a property personality, I realize there are limits to which each of us is able to go in changing our inner beings. And I also am aware of the wide variety of skills, temperaments and personalities among successful real estate investors whom I know personally. So I'm quite reluctant to make any gross generalizations about what the *sine qua non* may be for super success in this field.

What I will say, though, is that despite the fact that we've focused a lot on "riches" in this book, I don't think

that's the primary thing that motivates the most successful real estate entrepreneurs I know. At least, it's not what
motivates the happiest ones.

Oh, we all like to make money, and we like the com-
forts that money brings. Otherwise I'm sure we wouldn't
be in this field. But the investors I know who get the most
enthusiastic and who exult in the chase after a new property concept are the ones for whom big ideas, the promise
of adventure or some deeper spiritual commitment are
among the controlling features of their personalities.

As for me, I still love the excitement, the thrill of
"combat" with competitors and problems, or I wouldn't
stay in the business. And I would recommend the challenge of the "poor" or "rags" real estate market for anyone who has even the slightest inclination or talents in
that direction. It's really a lot of fun!

So I'm firmly convinced that it's necessary to work
hard and be a good steward of the hard-earned money of
others in these deals. And it's also important to maintain
a slightly playful, swashbuckling posture if you're really
going to enjoy yourself and stay loose enough to be a
success in this field. When you learn how to do it, making
money in depressed and overlooked real estate can actually be relatively easy, as well as fun and exciting.

After you capture a feeling of adventure about your
rags-to-riches property ventures and your unique property personality is well on its way to full bloom, you may
even be on your way to discovering what true *inner* riches
are all about.

Index